MW01602734

Hunting Big Woods Bucks Vol. 2

Hunting Big Woods Bucks Vol. 2

Hal Blood

WOODS N' WATER PRESS

© 2009 Woods N' Water Press, Inc.
P.O. Box 10, South New Berlin, New York 13843

ACKNOWLEDGEMENTS

My second book on hunting Big Woods Bucks would not have been possible without the support of all my fellow hunters and friends. Since writing my first book, I have had the opportunity to meet countless hunters who share the passion and mystique of hunting the most challenging of all whitetails. Thanks to all of you who have taken the time to share your experiences and compliments. To all of my guides at Cedar Ridge Outfitters, without your support and professionalism this business would not be possible. To the Ontario crew--I am blessed to be able to share a hunting camp with you. I treasure the memories and hope to make many more. Thanks to the guides who donated photos of them and their clients for this book. I can't thank Chris Dalti enough for joining in with me in making Big Woods Bucks a business dedicated to helping hunters learn the ways of these whitetails. His business skills and dedication to being a cameraman have enabled us to bring the woods to the hunter. Thanks again to Peter and Kate Fiduccia for their patience in getting me through another long project. Thank you Sue Morse, for the fine photographs you have contributed for this book. I can't thank my loving wife Deb enough. For without her running Cedar Ridge, I would never have the time for all the other things I need to do. As always, I need to thank the Good Lord for giving the health, guidance, and wisdom to get me through life.

Front cover, back cover and interior images by author. Additional images as noted, courtesy Sue Morse and Ted Rose.

To buy books in quantity for corporate, incentive or fund-raising sales, please email
booksales@fiduccia.com or call 1-800-652-7527

Published by: Woods N' Water Press, Inc.
P.O. Box 10
South New Berlin, NY 13843
www.woodsnwaterpress.com

Printed in the United States of America
10 9 8 7 6 5 4 3 2

Trade paper: ISBN-13 978-0-9820414-2-0 and ISBN-10 0-9820414-2-X
Hard cover: ISBN-13 978-0-9820414-4-4 and ISBN-10 0-9820414-4-6

TABLE OF CONTENTS

INTRODUCTION

I have known Hal Blood for more than 25 years. During that time, what has impressed me most about him is his penchant for speaking his mind. For instance, Hal is not one to promote a product if he feels it doesn't work to his satisfaction–which is one of the things that I admire about him.

What I respect most about him, however, is his unwavering commitment to his profession. Hal is a Master Maine Guide and he takes that responsibility very seriously. He is hard working and will give a 110 percent effort to each and every client he guides to help them end their hunt successfully.

But don't show up expecting Hal to baby you. That would be a mistake. When Hal is on the track of a buck he will dog it from sunup to sundown, up and down mountains, through bogs, tangles, woods and clear-cuts until he catches up with the buck, or has to abandon the trail. There is no middle ground for Hal when he's on the track of what he feels is a worthy buck.

Over the years I have produced our television show (Woods N' Water) I have been guided by hundreds of guides. I can frankly say that Hal Blood ranks as one of the most knowledgeable guides I know who has all the elements that make a guide not only skillful but, more importantly, successful.

Hal is not only an accomplished guide; he is an extraordinary woodsman who has learned over the years to become one with nature. More than that, he understands the behavior and tactics it takes to consistently bag one of the most difficult game animals in the woods, a mature, big woods buck.

Hal is not one to post in a treestand waiting for a buck to walk by, nor does he allow his clients to do so. While he does use deer calls and sometimes rattles, neither is within his usual comfort zone. Hal simply doesn't depend on most other commonly used deer tactics. Instead he depends on years of tracking experience and his uncanny abilities to get close to deer in big woods. Once Hal starts off on a track of a mature whitetail, the buck he is following is in deep poop. It had better draw on all its instinctive behaviors to evade one of the savviest, most experienced and talented big woods buck hunters this country has, or that buck will end up as a mount on someone's wall.

Hal is a no-nonsense type hunter, and he has no time to waste when on the track of a buck. He becomes so focused that he often sees, hears and even smells things that most other hunters–even experienced ones–will overlook. That makes him more than just a tracker; it makes him one of the most knowledgeable deer hunters in the nation.

Hal is the real deal. There are no facades or false pretenses about the hunt. He won't sugarcoat anything and he won't allow a hunter to give up. I strongly suggest that if you hunt with Hal Blood you better be ready to give whatever it takes, physically and mentally, to keep up with him. He is a tenacious pursuer and will wear down even the most physically fit hunters–some that are even years his junior.

Finally, when planning to hunt with Hal, make sure you have practiced snapping your rifle to your shoulder like it was an extension of your arm. Be prepared by having your head in the right place. Stay focused on the job at hand. When the time comes that Hal catches up with that big-bodied, mature whitetail big woods buck, things happen fast and often you only get one good opportunity for a shot. When you're hunting with Hal Blood, you are hunting elusive bucks, many of which have grown old though years of experience of evading lesser hunters.

Therefore, what you will take away from Hal's latest book is more than just a chance to read how to kill a buck on his own turf. You will learn how to become an all-around better woodsman and hunter from one of the most skilled professionals ever to enter the deer woods–a man who has justifiably earned the respect of countless deer hunters across North America.

Peter Fiduccia, aka The Deer Doctor, Host–Woods N' Water TV Series since 1983
Executive Publisher, Woods N' Water Press, Inc.

Bucks Without Rules

There is simply no other animal in North America more challenging to hunt than a Big Woods Whitetail Buck. After running an outfitting business and guiding service in northern Maine for almost 20 years, I have found that hunters either love to hunt in the big woods or they hate it. There doesn't seem to be any in-between. I've seen hunters quit and go home in the middle of their hunt and never heard from them again. I've also seen hunters stay in the woods to the last minute of their hunt and wish they didn't have to go home.

In either case, the big woods got to them. Some hunters are intimidated by it and some hunters embrace it. Any committed big woods deer hunter knows that it gets in your blood like an incurable disease. The disease got me 30 years ago and it is terminal. I just hope the good lord will give me another 30 years to pursue the bucks of the big woods.

Big Woods Bucks have evolved to be genetically larger-bodied deer.

The northern big woods buck is the largest-bodied of all white-tails. Bergman's rule says that the farther north a species of animal lives, the larger it will be. This rule takes into account the snow and cold conditions an animal has to endure. The more body mass a deer has, the more heat it carries, and therefore the less susceptible it is to cold. Only the big-bodied deer will survive extreme winters and then pass their genes along. Heavy-bodied deer can be found in a lot of places, but in the extreme northern part of the U.S. and in Canada, large-bodied deer are the rule. Bucks that field dress at more than 200 pounds are fairly common.

In the east you can follow the line that is the northern border of New York, Vermont and New Hampshire and continue that line through Maine and New Brunswick. South of that line there are very few bucks taken each year that field dress over 200 pounds. I've talked to some real good Adirondack buck hunters who have a wall full of trophy bucks and have never taken one that size. Even though the Adirondack Mountains are big woods, they are just not far enough north to produce big-bodied deer. North of that line is where a 200-pound buck becomes a likely occurrence.

Why do I say that a big woods buck is the most challenging buck to hunt? The simple answer is that they do not play by any rules. When I say rules, I'm referring to the rules that conventional deer-hunting wisdom has told us about how a buck behaves. Rule number one, we are told, is that a mature buck's home range will be three to five square miles. In the big woods, a yearling or two-and-a-half-year-old buck might have a home range that size, but a mature buck's home range can be two to four times that. I've tracked

A buck is always on the alert for danger. (Sue Morse photo)

2

bucks for four or five miles in one direction before they even started to make a circle. Those bucks were in their own territory and knew everything about it. They knew where every doe was and the easiest way to get to her. These bucks just simply like to roam.

I can remember finding a big buck track one morning where it had crossed a logging road. It was one of those zero-degree mornings during muzzle-loader season in Maine. As it turned out, the buck was lying within hearing distance of the truck and he got out of his bed and walked off while I was looking at his track. I was lucky to find a fresh track so early in the morning, but little did I know the journey that I would take that day.

First of all, the buck had been roaming all night and there was no telling how many miles he had come to get to where I picked up his track. When the buck left his bed, he traveled about three miles in a fairly straight direction before lying down again. It was a cold, still morning with only a couple of inches of snow, so I knew I was going to have a tough time trying to kill this buck. My good hunting buddy and guide, Mike Featherstone, was with me, carrying a video camera to record the hunt.

When we caught up to the buck, he had been feeding on some cedars and was laying down watching his back track. We jumped him out of his bed without seeing him. That's when the buck decided he wanted to return to where he had come from. He had been traveling in a southwesterly direction and had just turned back to the north.

Two hours later we were crossing the same logging road about three miles west of where we first picked up the track. We hadn't been able to get a look at the buck as the conditions were just too noisy in the thick cover where he was traveling. It was early afternoon by now, so I asked Mike to go back to the truck and drive north; I said I would see him at dark.

That buck continued north for the rest of the afternoon. I did see him twice but could not get the shot. When the buck crossed another old road near dark, we had traveled five or six miles in the same direction. I bid the old boy a farewell as I made my way back towards Mike and the truck.

When I returned home that night and looked at a map, I realized that the buck had taken me through an area of about 10 square miles and he wasn't even back to where he had come from. Big Woods Bucks are challenging to hunt as they can be eternal roamers. This roaming directly corresponds to the deer population density of any

This buck is making his rounds through the big woods. (Sue Morse photo)

given area. I have found that the lower the deer density of the area, the farther the bucks will roam.

I have been hunting the big woods of Canada for a number of years now. This has enabled me to understand the differences that big woods bucks have in different geographic areas. Western Canadian bucks do not roam as vast an area as eastern bucks do because the deer densities on average are greater in the west. Two things account for this: shorter winters and better winter habitat. The bucks in the west do not have to travel as far to find enough does to breed, so their home ranges tend to be smaller.

This brings us to rule number two: figuring out a buck's "pattern." In the deer-hunting world, patterning a buck refers to finding out where and when a particular animal is using or traveling through a certain area. Usually hunters focus their hunting in the area between where a buck feeds and where he beds down. In most places, the mature bucks have learned where to travel to avoid human contact. This usually involves them traveling in wooded strips between fields or brush-filled ravines. In any event, these bucks will continually use the same places on a daily basis as they travel to a food source.

Big Woods Bucks do not follow this rule either. Big woods are just that; there are no fields or agricultural crops to concentrate the feed. In certain areas and on certain years, there will be mast crops such as acorns, beech nuts and mountain ash berries. Deer are drawn to these foods sources, but they do not need to stay in one particular area as these foods will be spread throughout the woods. Combine this with his huge home range, and patterning a single big woods buck becomes an exercise in futility.

A big woods buck will continually adjust how he travels according to where the does are located. Does are more likely to concentrate around food sources that can change from year to year. I've gone into areas that held a lot of does one year only to find that they have moved to another ridge a half-mile away. This movement of the does will definitely dictate how a buck travels about.

A few years ago I spent some time hunting an area that a couple of bucks would pass through every day. It was a valley between two ridges with a small stream running through it. There were some old beaver flowages and cedar swamps all along the stream, and the whole area had been cut over in the past 10 years. There was a winter road where logging had taken place when the ground was frozen, between one ridge and the stream, and there were quite a few does there in the choppings, between the winter road and the stream. Every day the bucks would come down off from the ridge at the head of the valley and check on those does.

The following year I went back to that same area to hunt, expecting to find the same activity. As I worked my way up the valley, I could hardly find the sign of a doe using the area. Needless to say, the buck sign had disappeared, too, and that was my last day hunting that valley. After hunting for the rest of the day, I found the does on the other side of the ridge. I also found that the bucks were traveling on the top of the ridge instead of coming down into the valley.

All bucks are reclusive by nature and the big woods buck is no exception. Finding a reclusive buck in vast areas of unbroken forest is a challenge, to say the least. Most hunters assume that because the woods are so thick, a buck would not have to hide in an obscure, out-of-the-way place. A big woods deer's life is influenced not by man, but by predators. They are always on the alert for wolves, coyotes, bears, bobcats and mountain lions, depending on where the deer lives; they have learned to always watch their back trail and lay where nothing can approach them from behind. Bucks that adhere to these instincts will become big old moss horns.

Big woods bucks prefer to stay isolated from the rest of the deer. It's rare to find a mature buck bedded anywhere near other deer most of the time. I was scouting a couple of day before the deer season one year and was fortunate enough to have a little snow on the ground. I found some good buck sign that day and knew I would be returning to hunt there, so I decided to get out of the area the shortest way possible.

I soon found that the shortest way was not the easiest way out. I found myself down in a swamp and kept trying to circle to get around it. The woods were a combination of spruce thickets and cedar swamps, where the visibility was not very good. While making a circle, I came out to the edge of a beaver swale. Just as I stepped out I heard the telltale thump of a deer getting up. As I worked my way over to where I heard the sound, I began to see big buck tracks in the snow. By dumb luck I had stumbled onto one of those bucks hideouts. It was in a place that I would not have normally gone into if I was hunting, as it was just too thick for my liking.

The exceptions to the isolation rule are bucks that form a bachelor group during the summer and a buck that stays with a doe in estrus. He will push that doe away from any other deer and seek out a secluded spot where they can breed. Many times I have tracked a buck with a doe to some secret hideout that I would never have found otherwise.

Another rule that Big Woods Bucks break is about going to deer yards or wintering areas. Conventional wisdom is that deer move to their wintering areas when the snow gets deep, hampering their travel. Yarding areas typically have a canopy of conifers, mainly spruce, fir and cedar. These areas serve two purposes: the canopy keeps out some snow so it is not as deep and it also holds in a certain amount of heat to keep the deer warmer. Deer migrate to these areas from as far as 20 miles away. But as the demand for paper and wood has grown over the years, a lot of the traditional wintering areas have been logged off. In some cases the result has been that all the deer using that area die off from starvation and predation. In other cases it has forced the deer to crowd into ever smaller areas, where food is limited.

Some big woods bucks have adapted to this. They simply do not go to a yard. Instead, they choose to stay in some obscure place and tough out the winter alone. Over the years I have found bucks wintering in a variety of places, from the top of a mountain to a secluded cedar swamp. They do not move around much and typically will use the same bed all winter. They will venture out and feed a short distance from their bed and return to it to rest. These beds will become like a bathtub as the snow get deeper, helping to shelter them from the wind and cold.

Several times I have found a big buck hanging around with moose in the winter. They have learned to let the moose break out the trails in the snow that the buck can easily walk in. I think this adaptation has helped more mature bucks live through a winter that they might not have survived in a yard, where they would have had to compete for food.

Recently the whitetail deer has been expanding its range farther north in Canada, especially western Canada. There are no traditional deer yards in those areas, so the deer seem to make do wherever they are. I have found that these deer will bunch up in smaller groups where they have a softwood canopy and adequate food. I have also found that where there is cedar, the deer yard up in larger numbers. Yet some mature bucks still prefer to go it alone.

This buck will make sure his genes are passed on to the next generation. (Sue Morse photo)

7

As you can see, Big Woods Bucks do not follow the rules. This is what makes them the most difficult and challenging bucks to hunt. When you head for the big woods to hunt, you are going to be challenged in every way, but I guarantee that the reward will be well worth the effort. Once you master hunting big woods bucks, you will be in the top percentage of all hunters, qualified to hunt any game in North America. ❡

The life cycle begins all over again. (Ted Rose photo)

Unlocking the Secrets
of the Rub

There's something about a buck rub that gets a deer hunter's imagination running wild. Just seeing that bright spot on a tree, where a buck has shredded the bark off, conjures up images of how big a buck made the rub and what his antlers might look like.

Every deer hunter dreams or shooting a buck with thick, long beams and points that look like they came off a hay rake. All hunters have a fascination with any animal's antlers, and whitetail hunters are the most fanatical about them. In most areas of the whitetail's range, a hunter may get the chance to see a certain buck several times before the hunting season. Some hunters scout a particular buck by observing where he crosses a road or field. They may even watch the progress of a buck's antlers growing all throughout the summer.

In the big woods, it's whole different story. The odds of seeing the same buck twice, either before the hunting season or during it, are slim. There is just too much woods for a buck to roam. Of all the bucks I've actually shot in the big woods, not one had I ever seen before that hunt.

One year in Ontario, I'm sure that I saw the same buck twice. That buck had a big non-typical rack and was in the same clear-cut both times. I'm sad to say that buck is not hanging on my wall.

There was one time, though, that one of my hunters shot a 10-pointer that I believe I had seen two weeks earlier. I'd been scouting an area near one of my remote camps just before the season opened. It was near dark. I had come down off a mountain and was walking an old winter road when I stopped to look at a deer trail crossing the road. While I was looking down the trail to the left, I heard a crash to my right. I turned just in time to see a buck bounding away.

The first thing I noticed about that buck was his white antlers. Since most bucks' antlers in the area are golden brown, the white antlers really stuck out. The antlers also had quite a wide spread. My hunter shot his 10-pointer, with its white antlers and 20-inch inside spread, about a quarter of a mile away from where I saw that buck on the deer trail. It must have been the same buck.

Bucks rub trees for a variety of reasons. They also rub certain kinds of trees and in certain places. Rubs can tell us things about an individual buck, such as the size and shape of his antlers as well as if he is an older mature buck. By really studying the characteristics of a rub, a hunter will be able to piece together a buck's territory by finding his rubs. A buck may not always rub a tree in

This rub is on a brown ash but is not a signpost.

the same manner, but there still may be some clues that indicate a specific buck made a specific rub.

When I look at a rub, there are certain things that I'm looking for. The first thing is how far off the ground it is. The bottom of the rub may only be 12 inches from the ground, or it may start three feet off the ground. When a buck makes a rub, his neck is in a position that gives him the most power and leverage. This is a slightly downward angle from the top of his back. The taller a buck is, the heavier he is more likely to be. Since a rub will generally average about 24 inches from its bottom, its height off the ground tells us how tall a buck might be.

The next thing I look for is how much of the tree is rubbed. Quite often rubs are only six to eight inches from top to bottom, and such rubs don't' really tell us much. They could have been made by a small buck getting some practice or a big buck in a hurry making a few quick swipes at the tree. Trees that are rubbed one to two feet from the top to the bottom are usually made by a mature buck, especially if they are made on a larger diameter tree. Mature bucks are more aggressive by nature so they are more apt to really tear a tree up. If you look closely above the rub, you may see tine marks scratched in the bark. When they extend well above the top of the rub, it is an indication that the buck has long points or long main beams. If you find a rub that is two feet from top to bottom and the tine marks are a foot above top, it's safe to assume it was made by a really good mature buck.

The last thing I look at in a rub is how the bark is shredded and whether there are gouges in the surrounding wood of the tree. A rub that is fairly smooth would be an indication that the base of the buck's antlers has no burr points; most rubs you find will be of this typical smoothness. But a rub that shows cut marks in the bark or wood that has been cut into and splintered indicates a buck with burr points.

Burr points are just that: points that grow from the burr of the antler where it connects to the skull, and they usually occur as bucks get older or on bucks with antlers that are non-typical in fashion. I

The buck that made this rub had burr points and was most likely large and mature. (Sue Morse photo)

love finding these knurly kinds of rubs and trying to picture what the buck that made them looks like. Splintered wood could also mean that the buck has short brow points. But in any event the rub is most likely made by a mature buck.

Understanding how a rub is made will help you visualize what the buck that made it might look like. It will also help you distinguish one individual buck's rub from another. A buck does most of his rubbing at the base of his antlers between the burr and brow or first points. This is where he has the most leverage to bear down on the tree. At the base of a buck's antlers there are scent glands, and as a buck is making his rub he is depositing his scent on it.

A buck rubs in an up-and-down motion and will stop periodically to smell his rub. When a buck is rubbing his bases, he is strengthening his neck muscles in case he has to do battle with another buck in the future. By a buck making a rub head-on like this, we can also tell which direction the buck is traveling. Sometimes when making a rub bucks will use the back of their antler or maybe even their tines. Usually they do this on a small sapling or in the brush.

After studying rubs for so many years, I have broken them down into four different types. The four types are: Early, Traditional, Hookings and Signpost. Each type has certain significance, whether it is how, when or where it was made.

EARLY RUBS

Early rubs are made as soon as a buck loses the velvet covering on his antlers. Bucks shed their velvet in early September, exposing their brand-new antlers. When this happens, the buck will begin the process of polishing his new "crown of horns." The bone in these new antlers is not fully hardened, so a buck is careful about how he rubs them. These early rubs are usually made on small-diameter trees that will bend when a buck pushes on them. I find most of these early rubs on striped maple and poplar trees, which are softer and bend vary easily. Other trees or bushes early rubs can be found on are: willow, hazelnut, spruce and fir. Depending on the area you hunt, there may be other types of trees rubbed. No matter what tree the early rub is on, it will seldom be more than two inches in diameter. Usually early rubs are under an inch in diameter.

This early rub was made right after the buck shed his velvet. Note the mildew spots on the wood.

These parameters do not necessarily mean that the rub is an early one. There is only one way to tell for sure if the rub you're looking at is an early one. The exposed wood on the early rub will look faded and have black spots on it. These spots are caused by the tree sap mildewing. In September, when the early rubs are made, the temperatures are still warm enough to cause the sap to mold or mildew. Sometimes you will find quite a few of these rubs in a small area. That is because bucks don't move around as much that time of the year.

What can we learn from these early rubs? The truth is, not a whole lot, except that there has been a buck in the area. In fact, the

buck that made them may not frequent that area as much once he begins his fall travel pattern. The only time I pay much attention to these rubs is if there are other types of rubs in the same area. If I do find early rubs and other rubs in the same area, I know I have found key buck area. The biggest buck that I've taken so far was from such an area. You'll read the story about "Rackasaurus" later in the book. The importance of knowing how to identify these early rubs is so you can tell the difference between them and the other types of rubs.

TRADITIONAL RUBS

Traditional rubs are the most numerous and most common type of rub you will find. They come in all shapes and sizes and on all different kinds of trees. These are the rubs that will tell you the most about an individual buck. Once a buck polishes his antlers by making the early rubs, there is a period

Note the rubbings on two sides of the tree and the amount of shavings at the base. (Sue Morse photo)

of about a month when very little rubbing occurs. This seems to be true in every area of the big woods I've hunted. Bucks begin rubbing again in the pre-rut period or two to three weeks before the rut begins. In Maine I find very few rubs until the last week of October. In western Canada the rubs begin to show up about the second week of October.

Warm or cold weather can also influence the timing of when these rubs begin. Usually if I hunt in Ontario from mid to late October there are plenty of rubs and I find fresh ones every day. One year was exceptionally warm and there were very few rubs to be found. The whole time I hunted, the temperature was 50-60 degrees. At the same time back in Maine, they were getting snow and cold temperatures. That year there were more rubs than usual that last week of October.

Once a buck starts making traditional rubs, he will continue making them until his antlers are shed. There seems to be no rhyme or reason as to when and where a buck makes these rubs. They can be scattered about the woods anywhere a buck has traveled. The same buck may take the time to make a well polished rub two feet high or he may make a quick rub barely marking the bark on the tree.

What do traditional rubs tell us? They can tell us many things, from how many bucks are in the area to what a buck's antlers might look like and how big a buck might be. By studying these rubs you just might unravel the secrets that old "moss-horned" buck.

HOOKINGS

What I call hookings are made a little differently than the other types of rubs, generally on small scrubby trees or bushes. Most of the hookings I find are on willow brush. A buck does not spend much time making them. He will thrash his antlers around in the brush and rubs his bases very little. Since they are done quickly and not rubbed very much, they are the hardest rubs to spot. They also tell us the least about a buck. I usually find these hookings while I'm tracking a buck. I've tracked monster bucks that hooked the brush and the only way I noticed it was by seeing a few sprinkles of bark on the snow.

Tracking offers the best way to use hooking to your advantage. Most of the hookings are made just before or during the rut. I believe a buck makes them out of frustration, whether it's because he can't find a receptive doe or because he is with a receptive doe that is playing hard to get. I think all the guys can relate to this!

Tracking a buck that is making hookings while he's traveling along keeps me on high alert. A frustrated buck has let his guard down and will probably make some mistakes.

The first time I noticed this "frustrated buck syndrome" was one cold morning on the last day of the season. I had been tracking a good buck that was walking steady along a ridge and the track was frozen solid, so I wasn't wasting any time. The buck found a doe and followed her through a series of small grown-up clear-cuts. The doe had been feeding and the buck just kept hooking the brush all around her. I didn't count, but I would guess that he must have hooked 20-30 times in a 100-yard stretch.

I knew the buck would stay with the doe, but didn't expect him to lay in those cuts. I kept looking up the ridge at a green bluff and assumed that they would be up there. Boy was I wrong. That buck had let his guard down and was laying with the doe right in the cut. I was hurrying along on the track and didn't see them until it was too late. Another lesson learned and another buck that got away. He split from the doe and made no more mistakes that day. Hopefully someday I'll catch up to a frustrated buck with his antlers still in the willow brush.

SIGNPOST RUBS

Ever since I wrote about signpost rubs in my last book, hundreds of hunters have asked me more about them. Of all the rubs a buck makes, signpost rubs are by far the most important. They are not only the most important to us as hunters, but to the bucks themselves.

All animals communicate by scent and deer are no different. A signpost rub is established by a buck to communicate his presence to other bucks in the woods. He does this via his scent deposited on the rub. Unlike traditional rubs that a buck makes randomly, signpost rubs are made in specific locations within a buck's territory, usually in a secluded area where there is good cover, and generally where different bucks' territories overlap.

Sometimes more than one buck will use the same tree for a signpost and other times each buck will use his own tree in the same area. The most common misconception about them has been that all rubs on a brown ash tree are signposts. It's true that brown ash is the most common tree for a buck to make a signpost rub on in the Northeast. Every rub made on a brown ash is not necessarily a signpost, though. We'll get to that a little later.

So what really is a signpost rub and what makes it different from any other rub? Quite simply, a signpost rub is made on the same tree

Here is a sign post rub. Note the height of the rub when compared to the length of the author's rifle.

year after year. They are easy to identify if you take the time to look. When the bark is rubbed from a tree, it makes a dead spot on the tree. As the tree grows, the rubbed portion of the tree does not, which causes the tree to make a bulge at the rub as the bark tries to grow around the dead spot. As the tree gets older, the more pronounced this bulge will get. Then the dead area will begin to rot in the middle. Some of these signpost trees struggle to survive and will be noticeably smaller above the rub than below it. Sometimes the tree does die and usually another nearby tree is chosen to replace it.

This is the biggest signpost rub the author has ever found. It is almost two feet in diameter and has probably been rubbed for over 50 years.

Usually a signpost begins on a small tree between one and two inches in diameter. Once established, a buck will use it every year until he dies. When more than one buck is using the same signpost, it may be rubbed until something causes them to abandon the area. This may happen if logging takes place in the area and the woods becomes too open or active. I have seen many of my favorite signposts disappear for that reason.

One such signpost was on the edge of a ravine high up in a valley. If I was going to hunt that area, I always used it as a starting point. It was a two-mile walk on an old winter road to get back there. This particular signpost had seen years of use by numerous different bucks. I wondered how the tree could still be alive, as there was only about two inches of live bark left on it. Then one year a new logging road was built right beside the signpost and the whole area was cut off. To this day (10 years later), no buck has used that signpost.

Over the years I have found many signposts that I would guess to be at least 50 years old. The largest one I ever found was about two feet in diameter. Bucks were still rubbing the sides of the bulge, as they could not get their antlers around the tree. That signpost was in a high-elevation ravine close to the Canadian border. I discovered it by following an old buck to it. In that same ravine there were several other signposts within a 30-yard area. The snow was four days old when I found the place, and seven bucks had passed through the ravine in that time. Talk about a hotspot for bucks. If that tree could talk, I bet it would have some stories to tell! An area containing signposts that old and big are just natural places for bucks to travel. The only problem with this spot is that it is a three-hour walk from where I can drive to.

When a buck rubs on a signpost he is asserting his status in the area. Most of this rubbing is done in the pre-rut period, when bucks begin traveling more. The dominant bucks are the ones doing most of the damage to the trees, but even yearling bucks will visit signposts. Yearling bucks learn how to become big bucks by following the mature bucks around. I have a simple saying that makes it easy to relate: "Bucks go where bucks go." So if you are buck hunting, that's where you need to focus. You rarely see does around a signpost unless they are just passing by.

Unlike any other rubs, a buck may visit a signpost at any time, other than winter. Many times in the spring and summer, I have seen buck tracks at a signpost. Obviously they cannot rub the signpost with their velvet-covered antlers, but they do still rub scent from their foreheads on the trees. You have to look closely to see these subtle rub marks.

Bucks not only make their signpost rubs in specific areas, they also make the majority of them on specific types of trees–often on different species in different geographic areas. As I mentioned earlier, while brown ash is the most predominantly used signpost tree in the Northeast, in the big woods of western Canada the preferred tree is the willow. I have pondered on that for quite some time and have come to some conclusions. Unlike in the Northeast, where brown ash

This is a classic brown ash signpost. Note the discontinued one in the background.

grows in isolated areas, in western Canada brown ash or "black ash," as they call it there (which is really the true name), is commonly found everywhere. I think for that reason the bucks have chosen to make their signposts on the willow, which is far less common. My theory is that bucks choose to make signposts that will stand out in the crowd, so to speak. I also believe that using a particular type of tree for a signpost in any given area has been passed along by generations of bucks learning from other bucks. In any case, the trees that are chosen all seem to have one thing in common: their bark is soft and porous, which tends to hold the bucks' scent better.

Finding signpost rubs can be a challenge. As I've said before, bucks tend to make them in obscure, out-of-the-way places, where they feel the most comfortable. For that reason, signpost rubs are the most difficult rubs to find. I come across many of the signposts I see when I'm tracking a buck. But to find them on bare ground, you have to have some idea where to look.

Learn to identify the type of trees signpost are made on and it will make the search that much easier. Both brown ash and willow grow in wet areas. Knowing this, you should concentrate on looking around cedar bogs, beaver bogs and spring brooks. Rivers and streams are another good place to look, as bucks often make rubs at a crossing point.

The bud on the brown ash tree resembles little deer hooves.

Many of the hunters I talk to seem to have the most difficulty identifying the brown ash tree. I think one reason is that it is not too common in most areas. Another reason may be that it looks similar to its cousins, the white ash and green ash. But the bark of the brown ash is very different than the others. It is tan colored and soft to the touch. On younger trees the bark will easily crumble off when you touch it. Like all ash, the leaves of the brown ash grow from a stem instead of from the branch itself, as they do on most trees. In the fall the stems fall off along with the leaves, making the tree appear to be dead. If you look closely at the buds on the brown ash, they resemble little deer hooves, dewclaws and all!

As I've said before, signpost rubs are the most important buck sign to any deer hunter. They can reveal a buck's most intimate secrets. It doesn't matter whether you're a stand hunter, still hunter or tracker, using signpost rubs to your advantage will help you become more successful in the big woods. Learn to identify and find the signpost rubs where you hunt, and you will be well on your way to unlocking the mysteries of the Big Woods Buck.

This rub is a sign that a good buck is around.

Sometimes a buck will paw the ground while making a rub. (Sue Morse photo)

3

Making Sense of Scrapes

Of all the things relating to deer behavior, the "scrape" has probably been written about more than any other. Scrapes are the easiest buck sign to find. They stick out like a sore thumb, whether the ground is bare or covered with snow. There is no mistaking that patch of bare dirt where a buck has pawed out the leaves or snow with his front hooves.

There is something exciting about a scrape and there's a certain amount of wonder that goes along with finding it. We can clearly see the track of the buck that made the scrape and wonder how big he is and what he might have for antlers. We also wonder when that buck might be back to check that scrape again. We might wonder if we should sit here and wait, or if it is too late.

I'm not going to try and give you the science or biology behind scrapes, just my observations and interpretations of them and how you can use them to the best of your advantage in the Big Woods.

First of all, after looking at thousands of scrapes over the years, I have broken them down into three distinct types and given them my own names. There are: Annual Scrapes, Breeding Scrapes and Pawings.

PAWINGS

Pawings are the most common scrapes that you will find. A pawing is nothing more than a spot where a buck pawed the ground; it has no meaning as far as breeding purposes. I believe bucks make pawings in anticipation of the rut or, like hookings, out of frustration during the rut. A buck becomes frustrated that he can't find a hot doe or that a bigger buck has taken his doe away and he's looking for another one. Pawings may be made by a buck only taking two or three swipes at the ground, or they may be made by a dozen swipes. In either case they end up being small compared to the other scrapes, usually 12-18 inches wide and 18-24 inches long.

So what can we learn from pawings? The most important thing is the direction the buck is traveling. As a buck is walking along and stops to paw, he throws the dirt and leaves behind him.

Quite often a frustrated buck will walk along and paw the ground every 20 or 30 yards, which makes following him on bare ground fairly easy. I've found 15 or 20 of these pawings made by the same buck, stretched out across a hardwood ridge. I'll follow the pawings along to see if they take me to more buck sign and figure out where the buck might be traveling.

I can remember following one such buck on bare ground. He was kicking up dirt everywhere as he walked down off a ridge and into a cedar bog. Once I got into the bog, I started seeing brown ash. I knew there would be a good chance of finding some rubs, so my search began. It paid off with a signpost rub that I may have never found had I not been following that pawing buck.

The only other thing these pawings tell us is the size of the buck. If you look in the pawing you might see the buck's track and get an idea of his size. The buck that made those pawings may never go through that same spot again that season. He may not have found what he wanted in the area and will not return. So while it's exciting

Beaver bogs are good places to look for buck sign.

to see this buck sign, I don't put a lot of faith in just pawings, unless there are other reasons to keep me hunting there. It's a tendency for hunters to think that they've found a honey hole for bucks when they see what they think is a lot of scrapes in one area. Take the time to look at them and I think you might find them to be the pawings of one buck just passing through.

BREEDING SCRAPES

The next kind of scrape is the breeding scrape, the one that is talked about and written about the most. It's the classic scrape with an over-hanging limb. A buck will spend quite a bit of time making these scrapes. He will take care to paw out all the leaves and sticks from the area until the ground is bare dirt, and quite often he will urinate or defecate in the scrape to leave his scent.

These scrapes are usually two to three feet in diameter, although I have seen them five or six feet in diameter. Usually, when a scrape is that big, there are two or more bucks using the same one. The biggest scrape I have ever seen was made by three different bucks and was about seven feet wide and four feet from front to back. It was under a spruce tree and was almost a semi-circle.

You can tell if more than one buck is using the same scrape by looking to see where the dirt is thrown. Different bucks may come to the scrape from different directions, so if you see dirt on one side of the scrape thrown in one direction and the dirt on the other side thrown in another direction, there is more than one buck using it. Again the dirt is going to be thrown behind the buck in the direction he came from.

Another way to confirm that there is more than one buck is to look at the tracks in the scrape. Granted, different bucks can have the same size track, but quite often you can find some difference. Many hunters believe that a buck leaves his print in his scrape as a calling card, but logically it is just a coincidence indicating that he stood there after clearing the leaves out or marking an overhanging limb.

I find that a high percentage of these scrapes are made under soft-wood trees: spruce, fir, hemlock or pine. A breeding scrape will always have a tree limb or branch hanging over it. If the scrape does not have an overhanging limb, it is probably just a pawing. The limb overhanging a scrape is for a buck to mark with his own unique scent. Deer have scent glands on various parts of their body, and the one they use to mark the limb is located around their eyes. When a buck makes his scrape, he will actually spend more time placing his scent on the limb than it takes him to clear out the scrape itself. One time I had a hunter sitting in a ground blind watching a scrape. He told me that he watched a six-point buck come to the scrape and spend five minutes rubbing his eyes and smelling the limb over that scrape. It wasn't the buck he wanted, but the hunter witnessed something very few hunters get to see in the big woods.

I was tracking a buck one time on a dusting of snow that was just

Here is a typical breeding scrape with an overhanging limb.

beginning to fall. When I caught up to the buck, he was making a scrape. The buck was about 60 yards away behind a spruce tree. What caught my eye was one swipe of his front leg pawing out the scrape. I couldn't see the buck's body, so I waited for my chance to shoot. When a spruce limb began to shake, I could make out the buck's antlers and face. He didn't have a clue that I was around and I knew he had to step into the open, so I waited. It seemed like an eternity, as it always does when you're waiting out a buck, but it was probably more like two or three minutes. The buck was rubbing his eyes up and down the limb, pausing to smell it every so often. Finally, he turned and stepped into the open and I got my chance. That was the last step, that 10-pointer ever took.

The purpose of breeding scrapes is for a buck to send a signal to all the does in the area: "I am here and want to spread my genes." Conventional wisdom tells us that bucks make scrapes and then, when a doe is ready to breed, she will wait at the scrape of the buck of her choosing. The buck returns to check his scrape daily and finds a doe ready and waiting. That may be how it works in most of the whitetails range, but it is not necessarily how it works in the big woods.

Generally, big woods deer densities are much lower than other areas. Lower deer densities mean that a buck has to travel farther to find enough does to breed. I've hunted in places where there would be a mile between does. These are the areas where the bucks travel the farthest. It may be several days before a buck gets back to a scrape and even longer if he gets with another doe. Therefore does in the big woods do not hang around a scrape. They may visit a scrape to let a buck know that they are ready to breed, but then they just go about their business and let the buck find them. Finding an estrus doe is no problem for these bucks, as they already know where every doe in their territory lives. The bucks continually roam their territory, checking every doe in it until they find one that is receptive. They may or may not check all of their scrapes along the way.

Breeding scrapes are usually found in the vicinity of does. Sometimes this causes the scrapes to change locations from year to year as the does move to better feeding areas. Sometimes a buck will make a scrape where there were does living in the past. I don't know if this is wishful thinking or just habit. One time I tracked a monster buck about two through an area that looked like good deer country and never saw another deer track. The snow had been on the ground for four days and that was his first trip through there, so there couldn't have been many other deer around. The buck checked several scrapes along the way, so I figured there must have been does there at one time. That happened after a particularly harsh winter, so the does from that area could have died off. Where ever you find a breeding

This scrape has been here for years. Note the fresh limbs in the scrape and old broken limbs on the tree.

scrape, the buck that made it will eventually be back.

ANNUAL SCRAPES

The third type of scrape is the annual scrape–actually nothing more than breeding scrapes that are made in the same place year after year. These scrapes are generational and will be taken over by a different buck once one has died off. They may also be used by more than one buck at a time. They are made along a buck's travel route where there have traditionally always been does, which is where the term "scrape line" came from.

There are a couple of ways to tell if you have found an annual scrape. First look at the ground where the scrape is made. The ground is usually dished out like a bowl from the dirt being pawed out over the years. This is especially true if the scrape is under a softwood tree where there are only needles to cover the scrape instead of leaves. Also look in the scrape to see if there are any tree roots. These will have hoof marks on them from being pawed in previous years. Now look at the overhanging limb. You should be able to see where parts of the limb have been snapped off in the past. This is easy to see, especially on spruce or fir trees, which are more likely than other trees to have multiple limbs branching out. I have found scrapes where the bucks had broken off 10-15 limbs and branches over the years. These scrapes are important to the hunter as, like a signpost rub, they tell you that bucks have always traveled there and probably always will.

Now that you know what a scrape is, where and why they are made, I'll give you a couple of observations I've made and the conclusions I've drawn from them as they relate to the big woods.

There seems to be a direct correlation between the number of scrapes in an area and the number of does. Contrary to what one might think, there are more scrapes when there are fewer does. My theory is that when there are fewer does, the competition for them among bucks is greater. After a series of easy winters, which allows the deer population to grow, a buck has no problem finding an estrus doe once the rut starts. There are also plenty of does to go around for all the mature bucks. Therefore a buck doesn't find it necessary to make as many scrapes around the does.

I observed this happening over about a 10-year period in northern Maine. In the late '90s there were several hard winters in a row. The deer herd in a lot of areas was knocked down to fairly low numbers per square mile. During that time there were always plenty of scrapes

in the woods during the fall. After those winters there were six rela-
tively easy winters in a row. During those years there was very little
winter kill other than by coyotes. The deer herd rebounded and, at the
same time, the number of scrapes decreased. It was perplexing, to say
the least.

This buck is depositing his scent on the limb over a scrape. (Sue Morse photo)

I remember a couple of different years when I guided a hunter all
the first week of the season and never saw a scrape. Sometimes it was
hard to convince hunters that there were actually plenty of bucks in
the area. Those were the times when I relied on the signpost rubs to
keep a client's interest up. Every hunter I talked to would mention the
lack of scrapes in the woods and ask me my opinion on it. At the time
I was just as perplexed as anyone else about it. During that time, I
tracked bucks day after day and many times they would never make
a scrape. It seemed almost impossible to me that a mature buck would
travel 10 miles or more checking does along the way and never stop
to make a scrape.

Then came the winter of '07, when all of the North and especially the Northeast had a record-breaking winter. Snowfall records were
being broken everywhere. Parts of northern Maine got up to 200
inches of snow. Every one of us deer hunters was concerned for the
deer, knowing that most deeryards were marginal at best. Some areas
lost well over half of the deer herd that winter. Deer numbers were

down everywhere, especially does and fawns. The fawns are always the first to succumb to a harsh winter. Their small size doesn't allow them to reach high enough to compete for what little food is available. They also cannot carry enough fat reserve to offset the lack of food. Does are the next to succumb, as they have to supply not only food for themselves, but for the fawns they are carrying.

The deer in the areas I hunt fared better than most places in northern Maine, but the doe population had definitely decreased. When I began scouting for deer that spring, it seemed as though there were still plenty of bucks that had made it through the winter. I really confirmed it when I began fall scouting the week before the deer season opened. As I began checking some favorite places, I found fresh scrapes, and lots of them. I couldn't believe what I was seeing. It was like a return to the old days. My first thought was how could there be that many more bucks. The number of scrapes increased all throughout the season. The only conclusion I could come to is that with fewer does in the woods, the bucks were once again in competition for them.

Another observation I've made is that a buck doesn't freshen-up a scrape every time he checks it. I have found scrapes that were made early in the season and never freshened again. This doesn't mean a buck has not been by. Time and time again I have tracked a buck that walked right through scrape after scrape and never bothered to freshen one. Other times a buck might just make a few quick paws at it. This usually happens once the rut has started. Then the bucks are either with a doe or looking for one.

Once snow covers the ground, a buck is more likely to freshen-up his scrapes again. I don't know if it's because the snow has covered his scent or that maybe the bare dirt of a scrape is also a visual clue to a buck's presence. Scrapes are one of bucks' many calling cards and there are many ways to use them to your advantage, so study them and learn them.

Hunting from a ground blind shelters a hunter from the weather and allows for some movement.

4

Choosing the Best Stand Location for Success

S tand hunting is a very successful way to hunt in the big woods. It allows a hunter who may not be able to walk the distances necessary to track and still hunt the opportunity to hunt in the big woods. It also gives the hunter another option when the conditions are poor for tracking or still hunting.

Stand hunting in the big woods is far different than in agricultural type areas, for a variety of reasons. The number one reason is that there is so much territory for a buck to travel in that he could be anywhere on any given day. This requires stand hunters to have the patience to stay in their stands day after day, all day, no matter what the conditions.

Unlike other areas, where stand hunting is a morning and evening event, in the big woods you are just as likely to shoot a buck in the middle of the day. The stand hunter is also going to have to do the proper scouting to ensure a good stand location. From my experience, a big woods buck spends most of his time traveling through 10 percent of his territory. In this

This buck was taken from a ground blind while watching a scrape.

33

chapter, I'm going to try and help you figure out where that 10 percent is. We'll also explore ways to capitalize on those areas no matter what time of the season you hunt.

There are several types of stands locations that are effective in the big woods. There are certain times that one specific stand location may be better than another, and they can also vary from year to year. By having stands in several different locations, you will be able to maximize your odds of seeing a buck. Too many hunters pick a stand location just because it looks like a good area, or because they have good visibility there. In the big woods there are a lot of good-looking places that have not had a deer pass through them in years. Stand hunting in some of these areas will become an exercise in futility and the odds of shooting a buck are somewhere between slim and none. In my first book, I talked mostly about pre-rut and rut stands. I am going to expand on those types of stands by breaking them down into four basic locations. They are: Pre-Rut, Rut, All-Season and Migration-Trail stands.

PRE-RUT STANDS

In the pre-rut period, bucks for the most part are just getting ready for the rut. They've had all summer to fatten up and now they know the chance to spread their genes will soon be here. The bucks are laying down scrapes and rubs throughout their whole territory. They are crossing paths with other bucks and making a point to announce their presence by marking signpost rubs with their scent.

I believe sitting over a signpost rub, especially if more than one buck is using it, is the most effective pre-rut stand. Since most of the signposts are made in obscure, out-of-the-way places, a buck is more likely to show up there during the day. If there is a breeding scrape near a signpost, it makes the stand location even that much better, as there are most likely does in the area. Keep in mind that a mature buck has a huge territory and is not going to pass through the same area every day.

One such signpost area that I had found I passed off to Matt Whitegiver, one of the guides working for me, so he could put up a stand there. I wasn't hunting that area anymore as it had grown up too thick to be very good for still hunting. There were plenty of deer around and I knew a stand hunter would have a good chance of taking a buck there.

This particular place was at the back corner of a hardwood chopping. The chopping had grown up with raspberry bushes and saplings. Bordering the chopping on two sides was an old grown up softwood clear-cut and cedar bogs. Just inside the softwoods, at the corner of the chopping, were several signpost rubs. There were also a couple of scrapes in the corner of the chopping.

Matt put up a ground blind with the intention of having a hunter there for the first week of the season. The hunter that was going to hunt this spot had brought a treestand and wanted to use it instead of the ground blind. Matt carried the treestand in the first morning and the hunter climbed up in it to sit for the day. When the hunter came out of the woods at the end of the day, he told Matt that he had seen 13 does. Matt told the hunter that he had seen more deer in one day than most people see in a week.

The next day the hunter didn't see a single deer from his tree-stand, and told Matt he wasn't going to go back there. Even I couldn't convince the guy to stay in that stand. Talk about trusting your guide! The next day Matt moved the hunter to another stand. The hunter's treestand was still at the first place, so at about noontime Matt decided that he might as well go in and bring the stand out. As he was heading in he spotted a deer walking down by the stand. He stopped and waited to see what it was. It turned out to be a nice eight-point buck and it walked right under the treestand. I guess sometimes lessons have to be learned the hard way.

I've learned that there is a different dynamic to stand hunting in the big woods of northern Canada. This area is a mostly a coniferous forest that contains very little feed for deer, with the exception of some isolated cedar bogs. In fact, most of these areas didn't contain any deer until they were logged. Most of the logging has been by clear-cutting and has created a vast amount of feed for deer by letting in sunlight so new plants can grow. The logging has allowed deer to expand into new areas.

Even though it is big woods, the habits of the deer around clear-cuts are more like that of farm-country deer. You have to view the clear-cuts almost as you would agricultural fields and not like most big woods areas, where there is feed almost anywhere. The only other places that contain much feed for the deer around these coniferous forests are near the swale bogs where sunlight has allowed the feed to grow. Unlike the big woods bucks of the east, bucks in these areas tend to travel the same trails as the does do.

In areas with a lot of these clear-cuts, the best stand locations are in the cuts that are not visible from a road. This might be the back of a cut that is hidden from the road by a knoll or it might be a cut that has no drivable road to it. Lee Libby found one such place on a cold rainy morning in Ontario.

Lee was sick with a cold that morning, so when the other guys got out of the truck to hunt they told him that he should sit in the vehicle until the rain stopped. Lee, being Lee, couldn't stand to be in the truck, so he decided to hunt his way to the back of a clear-cut that was grown up with head-high jack pines. He worked his way down the old road leading into the cut. When the road ended he couldn't see 20 yards, so he walked up onto a ledge to look for a better view of the cut. From the ledge he could see several hundred yards down into a ravine that ran to the back of the clear-cut. Lee hadn't been standing there very long when he spotted a good buck standing on the other side of the cut, about 200 yards away. At the sound of Lee's muzzle loader going off, the buck dropped in his tracks. When Lee got over to the buck, he discovered that he had shot a beautiful 14-pointer.

Later in the season, Mike Featherstone's friend Dave shot another buck in the exact same spot. What made this a good stand location was that, at the back of the clear-cut, there was a buffer strip of woods that dropped down a steep ridge into a lake. That made it difficult for the deer to go around the cut. Those two bucks had been using that hidden ravine to cross the clear-cut as they traveled along the lake.

Some clear-cuts are used heavily by deer and others are not. You will have to check for feeding sign while scouting. Quite often these clear-cuts border a swale. These grassy swales are created when the beavers flood an area and kill all the trees. When the clear-cuts border a swale, there is usually a strip of woods between the cut and the swale called a buffer strip. By walking the back of the clear-cuts, you can usually see if there is a swale behind it.

Swales have good stand locations around them. They can run for miles, so deer have to cross them at some point. Quite often the crossings will be at a narrow point in the swale. Deer also like to cross where there is a corner in the swale. It is easy to spot these crossings in the swale grass by walking along the edge of it and looking for the bent-over grass. If there are rubs or scrapes at these trail crossings, you've found an excellent location for a stand.

RUT STANDS

Once the rut begins, the only thing a mature buck has on his mind is breeding. This is going to make it impossible to predict when and where he may be at any time. The best chance of seeing a buck from a stand now is by hunting around the does. If you have a stand by a

Guide Lee Libby with his 245-lb. 14-pointer taken while watching a travel corridor in the back of a clear-cut in Ontario.

signpost rub with a breeding scrape near it, the odds of seeing a buck there are very good. However, some of the obscure signposts in a buck's territory may not get visited once the rut starts. I've checked on some signposts during the rut while looking for a buck track to follow, without seeing a track on week-old snow. Not to say that a buck won't pass by a signpost, but the ones they do pass by will probably be between the areas where there are does.

I feel the best stand locations during the rut are near does, and the does in any area may move from year to year, depending on the food source. This means that you have to find the hardwood ridges or choppings that the does are using. The more does that are in an area the

Gene Nygaard shot this 205-lb. eight-point while stand hunting a doe area at a Cedar Ridge remote camp.

better, as the odds of one of them being in estrus at any given time is greater. Every buck within miles will be checking on the does that they know are there, and you should be able to find a breeding scrape in an area where there are does. This scrape should be the prime location for your stand. Make sure you pick a good vantage point, where the wind will be in your favor.

This is a great time to use some doe-in-estrus scent. One way to use this scent is to put it on scent pads for your feet and use them when you walk to your stand. There is a chance that a buck might cross your trail and follow the scent right to you. If you don't have any scent pads, you can attach a small piece of rag to a string and tie it around your ankle so it drags on the ground behind you. Another way to use estrus scent is to either hang a dispenser or spray it on a limb downwind of your stand. Make sure you have a clear shooting lane to the scent, as a buck will most likely stop there to smell it.

ALL-SEASON STANDS

There are certain stand locations that are effective at any time of the season. These locations are usually associated with natural travel corridors, such as ridge saddles, stream crossings or other terrain features. The best way to find a potential stand location is to study a TOPO map of the area. Look for steep ridges that have saddles through them. The longer and steeper the ridge is, the better, as it will funnel more deer through the saddle.

Deer travel for the most part by taking the path of least resistance and following the natural flow of the terrain. They also tend to cross streams where the water is shallow. Shallow water moves faster and creates a riffle which is less likely to freeze in cold weather. One day late in the season, I was tracking a buck along a ridge above a small stream. I knew there had been a doe staying near the end of the ridge, and when I got there, I could see buck tracks were everywhere. I circled the area and found four different buck tracks leaving it, all going in the same direction. All of the buck tracks had been made the night before, and they had all checked on the doe. When the bucks dropped down into a flat along the stream, they all converged on the same point to cross the stream. The stream was frozen except for about 10 feet of fast-moving water where the bucks crossed, and the stream bank was cut back from years of deer crossing there. The combination of the flat along the stream and the shallow water made this a natural place for deer to cross and a great place for a stand.

Finding good stand locations is helpful for the still hunter or tracker. They can be used for stopping points when still hunting or a place to look for a buck track to follow. One year I was scouting an area that I had found the previous year. I found the area while tracking a buck through it, and there was enough good sign to warrant going back. I was fortunate enough to have a little snow on the ground when I went back to do some scouting. I cut a good buck track that was a couple of days old coming down out of a saddle. The track turned along a steep hardwood ridge and intersected another buck track that was going in the opposite direction. As I looked down the other track, I could see a scrape. Twenty yards away from it, there was another scrape. I could see that this ridge was funneling the bucks around it and thought it would be a good place for a stand.

I continued on the tracks until they came to the end of the ridge, and I realized that it was the spot where the buck I tracked the year before had gone. It was an intersection of two buck trails and I was thinking that this could be a real hotspot for a stand. There was a little shelf that stuck out from the ridge that would make a good ambush point. I decided this was going to be one of my taking-a-break or sandwich spots when I was in the area.

I didn't get back into that spot until the third week of the season that year. There was a dusting of snow on the ground and I was tracking a buck with a client. We had picked the track up about a mile away and followed it off the end of the ridge to the trail intersection. The buck then went down in the low ground where there was no snow. It was getting to be sandwich time, so we went up to the little shelf to take a break. We spent an hour there and continued on our hunt.

The next week I was hunting for myself with a cameraman named Rob Wing, and I decided to try that area again. I picked up an average-sized buck track that morning on crusty snow. I followed the buck around a swamp as he checked on some does. The buck finally headed up a ridge and started following the track of a monster buck that had been there the day before. Both of the bucks were headed back along the ridge toward the swamp. I decided to hunt toward the little shelf, which was about a half-a-mile away, in hopes of finding a better track to follow. I was thinking that a buck might have come out of the saddle in the steep ridge, but no such luck.

Once again, I decided to take a sandwich break on the shelf. Rob and I went up on the shelf and kicked out a place to sit where we could watch both trails. Once I sat down, I realized I couldn't see down into the hardwood ravine. I thought about moving over, but figured anything coming through the saddle would come around the shelf. Boy did I call that one wrong.

We had been sitting there about half an hour and I was just getting my cookies out when Rob said he could here crust breaking in the ravine. I got up on one knee and spotted a deer walking along about 100 yards away. I took out my binoculars and got them focused just in time to see a tall-tined buck pass between two trees. I brought my gun up, but couldn't get a shot, as now all I could see were flicks of brown as the buck disappeared into the green growth. Had I only followed my instincts and moved over to where I could see in the ravine, I would have seen the buck coming from over 100 yards away. The buck had come down out of the saddle, right where we had just checked for tracks. Oh well, that's the way it goes. But at least it proved to be a good stand and I know I'll be there again.

Sometimes a good stand location requires a long walk to get to it. Other times you might find a good location close to or where a buck is crossing a gravel road or winter road. Bucks tend to avoid roads with a lot of activity as much as possible, especially during the day, but in some areas there are just too many logging roads to avoid them.

Usually these road crossings are in travel corridors between terrain features where bucks have always traveled. There is a place like this in one of my remote camp areas.

When they logged the area about 10 years ago, they built a road between a steep ridge and a swale bog. The road ended in line with the end of the bog and just beyond where the ridge ended. There was a brushy ravine crossing the road with ledges on the backside of it, and a flat area about 75 yards long between the ravine and the end of the steep ridge that was a natural travel corridor. Over the years, we had tracked plenty of bucks across the road at that spot. The second week of the season one year, Mike Featherstone had some hunters who wanted to stand hunt. He told one of them to put his treestand up where he could watch this crossing. Mike drove off and the hunter put his stand up and climbed into it just as it started to snow. Fifteen minutes later, the hunter spotted a buck making his way up to the road. He said the buck looked both ways and stepped into the road. One quick shot and that hunter had himself the Big Woods Buck of his dreams. That story proves that being in the right place at the right time is everything!

MIGRATION-TRAIL STANDS

Deer use migration trails to get to their wintering areas. These trails can be miles long, and the closer to the yard they get, the more use they will see. When the snow begins to get deep and temperatures drop to near zero degrees for an extended period, the deer will start moving toward their yarding area by following these age-worn trails. Usually this migration takes place in early December, but occasionally it will begin in late November. When it does, these trails are a great place for a stand hunter to set up. Does and fawns are typically the first to go to the yards, but mature bucks that may not otherwise go to a yard will follow a doe in estrus to it.

Migration trails can sometimes be the most productive stands of all. They are easy to find and identify, once they start being used. All but an occasional track in the migration trail will be going in the same direction. Usually a track going in the opposite direction is a buck searching the trail for a doe or going back to where he came from.

The easiest way to find a migration trail is by driving logging roads. Once you locate a crossing, check your map to see if there may be another road in the direction the deer are coming from. Try to find the largest area of woods that the deer are coming from so there is less of a chance another hunter is set up on the same trail. Another good place to look for migration trails is along streams and around lakes or ponds. These are natural places for them, as there is usually softwood cover that keeps the snow depth down.

You may find a migration trail while hunting on bare ground without realizing what it is. If you find a well-worn trail in the woods that doesn't appear like it's being used very much, there's a good chance that it's a migration trail. Hundreds of deer use these trails every year to get to and from the yard, causing the trails to get worn into the ground. Other than that, these trails see very little use. I've checked migration trails week after week during the season without ever seeing a track. Then, once the migration starts, there will be new tracks on them every day. You may not be able to use a migration-trail stand every year, but the years you can could be productive ones.

UP YOUR ODDS

Stand hunting is also a good time to try calling deer. Calling can increase your chances of seeing a buck, as you may be able to lure one that is passing out of sight back toward your stand. Obviously, calling is not going to work every time it's tried, but I've seen it work enough to know it helps tip the odds in your favor. It also helps to pass the time when you're spending a long day on stand.

Rattling is most effective during the pre-rut period. It is well suited to hunting in the big woods by virtue of the sound carrying the farthest of any calls. When deer densities are low, the farther the sound of a call carries, the more likely a buck will hear it. One year at Cedar Ridge, three of the hunters in camp rattled in good bucks in one week. Two of the bucks were put on the pole and the third buck was missed. I wasn't very far away from one of the hunters, so I got a firsthand account of what happened.

Lee Libby and I had been guiding our clients in the same area. Lee had a father and son, both named Gary, and I was guiding one of my regular clients, Sue Morse. Gary Tiso (senior) had missed the buck he rattled in from his treestand on Tuesday. Thursday morning was clear and cold with about an inch of snow on the ground. Lee set up Gary junior against the root ball of a blown-down tree, where he could watch a logging road. There had been a good buck crossing the road quite frequently near two grown-up clear-cuts, so Lee figured this spot would be a good bet. Sue and I decided to sit for a while that morning in a ravine where we had found some good buck activity the day before. We hadn't been sitting there long when a shot rang out in the distance. About five minutes later, two more shots echoed through

Gary Tiso rattled in this 205-lb. eight-point in the pre-rut at a Cedar Ridge remote camp.

the cold, still air. The shots had come from Gary junior's direction, so I decided to go check on him.

I walked the half mile back to the truck and drove toward Gary, not knowing at the time exactly where he was sitting, but just driving along and looking for footprints going into the woods. I spotted him standing beside the root ball, 30 yards off the road. He said he'd shot a buck and pointed at the ground behind him. When I asked him if he had called Lee on the radio, he told me that in his excitement, he had dropped the radio in the water and it wasn't working. I got my radio out and called Lee to tell him Gary had shot a buck. While we were waiting for Lee to get there, Gary told me his story.

He said Lee put him in a chair against the root ball for cover, with a good view of where the buck had been crossing the road. As soon as Lee left to put his father on stand, Gary did a rattling sequence and settled in for the wait. He said about 15 minutes later, he heard a stick snap behind him. He knew it must be a deer, so he turned his head to peek through the roots.

Gary said he couldn't believe his eyes when he saw a nice eight-point buck walking right towards him through the whips. He eased his gun up over the roots just as the buck stopped, about 30 feet away. Gary said all he could see was the buck's head above the whips–and at the shot the buck dropped dead in his tracks. That buck had pin-pointed the rattling and it didn't take him long to get there.

Buck grunting as well as doe bleating can also be effective when sitting on stand. There are so many different calls on the market today that trying to pick the right one can be overwhelming. Not all deer sound alike, so not all calls have to sound alike. Using a call proper-ly is far more important than the brand of call you use. To be effec-tive at calling you have to learn what sounds to make in certain situations. I don't consider myself an expert deer caller, as I don't sit on stand to practice it enough. Most of the calling I do is to tip the odds in my favor while tracking and still hunting. I still rely on my trusty old Alaskan deer call, but they are not made anymore. If you want to learn how to call deer effectively, I suggest you contact Peter Fiduccia, at Woods N' Water, Inc. (See Appendix for contact informa-tion.) Peter, who has been calling deer for over 40 years and is, in my opinion, the foremost authority on the subject, says that to call deer effectively you have to "create the illusion." His books and DVDs will help you to learn the proper calls for every situation.

QUICK STANDS

Sometimes a stand made quickly or at the spur of the moment can pay off in places where circumstances tell you to take a stand there. It might be some hot doe activity you stumbled across or some new buck sign that piques your interest. A stand doesn't have to be an elaborate set-up; it might just be some boughs thrown down on the ground so you can sit against a tree. Don't be afraid to take a chance on a hunch, as sometimes hunches can change your luck.

One of my guides, Tom Hamilton, had his hunters sitting in an area that I had been moose hunting in that fall. I told Tom that I'd found where a couple of different bucks were hanging around some new choppings.

Tom decided to scout around in that area the next day and found a good scrape line through one of the choppings. He brushed up a quick ground blind, with the intention of putting a hunter in it the fol-lowing day. It snowed in the night and Tom took a hunter into that stand shortly after daylight the next morning. Not long afterwards, a nice eight-point buck came along, opening up his scrapes again. That was the last trip that buck made through his territory.

There are many different types of stands a hunter can use, including commercially made ladder stands as well as portable climbing and hang-on stands. There are also pop-up tent type blinds that are good for blocking the wind and keeping your scent from dispersing.

The type of woods and terrain you're hunting will dictate which stand or blind is the best choice for the area. The type of stand you use will also depend on how far back in the woods your stand location is. If it is a good walk in, you may prefer to go with a blind made from natural materials around the area. Ground blinds can be made as simple or as elaborate as you choose.

But no matter what type of stand you decide to sit in, the proper location for it is far more important than the stand itself.

A ladder stand is quick and easy to get into and it gives a hunter the advantage.

This buck is scent checking (flehmening) for any does that might be coming intro estrus. (Sue Morse photo)

Accomplishing the Art
of Bare-Ground Hunting

Hunting on bare ground in the big woods can sometimes seems like a daunting task. Deer densities are lower than in farm country, making it more difficult to find and hunt them. The mystique and challenge of hunting bucks in the big woods is what compels us to do it, no matter what the odds. The time of the season, weather, terrain and deer densities all determine the best way to hunt on any given day. I have learned the tactics and techniques in this chapter through trial and error while hunting the in big woods over the last 30 years. I hope these tactics work for you as well as they have for me and you find that buck of your dreams.

SCOUTING

Scouting is the most important thing that a hunter must learn to do. If you do not know how to scout the big woods for deer, you are probably going to have a difficult time finding deer to hunt. Deer are not dispersed evenly throughout the big woods. They will be found in select areas, where the feed and cover suits them the best. I've been in areas of northern Maine where there was very little deer sign for miles. I have also found areas that may contain as many as 10-15 per square mile. As a general rule, the closer to a deer-wintering area you are, the higher density deer there will be.

When I started hunting in Ontario, I found the deer density to be quite a bit higher than in Maine overall. But even so, there are still many places that contain very few deer. One time I decided to hunt a large area between a road and a clear-cut. It was about two miles through this piece of woods and I had high hopes of finding some good bucks in there. We had hunted around the clear-cut before and knew there were plenty of deer there. We had also quite often seen deer crossing the road.

Chris Dalti was following me with the camera as we headed in from the road that morning. There was some deer sign, but not really what we had expected. About half a mile back in we came to a swale with some fresh rubs on the alders. As we eased up the edge of the swale, a six-point buck jumped up and bounded across the swale and stopped. We watched him for a few minutes before working our way around the swale. We hunted all around the swale, but couldn't find any really big buck sign. I thought maybe the farther in we hunted, the better the sign would get. Boy, did I turn out to be wrong.

We crossed the swale and walked through moss-covered ledges and jack pines for the next mile and a half without seeing any indication that a deer had been around. Then I began to realize that there just was not any feed to keep the deer in the area. If you don't do the scouting, you will never know.

My first step in scouting is going over a map of the area I'm interested in. I usually do this in the doldrums of winter as I daydream about those old moss-horned bucks. I study the maps to learn the terrain and the location of water, which gives me a good idea of where the deer may be and where the bucks might travel. Lakes, rivers and steep ridges are natural barriers to deer. They normally take the path of least resistance when travel-ing. It's not natural for them to go straight up a steep ridge or swim a lake or river. They will do it, but it's the exception, not the rule. A map will show me these things so when I get ready to go in the woods, I will have a good idea of where to start looking for sign.

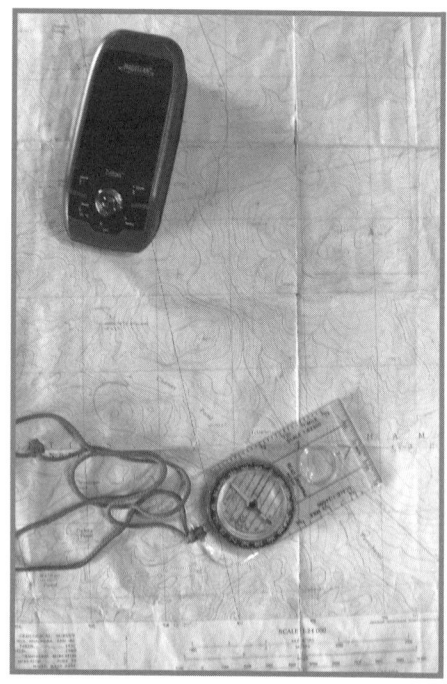

The two things I want to find out when I'm scouting are how many does are in the area and where the buck sign is. Typically speaking, if there are does in the area, there will be buck sign around. But quite often there will be a lot of buck sign even when there are no does around. If that's the case, I know it will be a good pre-rut area to hunt.

A map and compass are essential for hunting the Big Woods.

I do some of my scouting in the spring, as soon as the snow leaves the ground. In the spring everything still looks the way it was before the snow covered it for the winter. Scrapes will still be evident, as will the rubs, before the sun has had a chance to fade them out. Most hunters think the fall is the best time to scout for deer. Unless you wait at least a week after the leaves have fallen off the trees, there will be very little deer sign to see. As the leaves fall, they cover any tracks and droppings as though it were snowing. Even when scouting an area that may contain a lot of deer, it may be discouraging.

I do a lot of scouting while I'm hunting. I choose days when I feel there will be less chance that a buck might be roaming around for my scouting/hunting opportunities. Usually these are the warm sunny days earlier in the season and before the rut. I start my scouting by following a stream or spring brook. I walk along these waterways where I feel a buck is most likely to travel, such as in the transition between green growth and hardwoods. These edges are a good place to find signpost rubs.

I look for tracks or trails that parallel or cross the stream. If I find a good crossing, I may follow it to see where the deer are going or I may just continue along the stream. I make these decisions as they present themselves. At times, I may follow a stream for miles and other times I will walk up a ridge in hopes of finding a trail along it or some sign that there are does in the area.

If I'm going up a ridge, I usually try to follow a spring seep coming off the ridge because I am more likely to find a signpost in the wet ground around a seep. Any place along a ridge that has a saddle, there should be deer activity. Saddles are natural crossing areas for deer to get from one side of a ridge to the other. No matter where I travel, I'm always looking for rubs and scrapes so I can try and piece together how the bucks are traveling the area.

When I scout, I move along at a pretty good pace. I want to be able to cover as much ground in a day as I can and I'm looking to find deer sign as much as I am deer. When I do find good sign, I will slow down and spend some time in that area before moving along again.

There have only been a few areas that I have scouted where I did not find deer sign if I walked far enough. One of these areas, though, was a big disappointment. I had been looking over this area on the maps for a couple of years before finally getting the chance to scout it. It was one of the few big roadless places in the whole area and it had just being opened up by logging. Since the area was quite a distance from home, I decided to do my scouting in the spring so I could make a remote camp there if it looked good enough.

I drove to a spot where I could walk up a small brook between two big ridges. Right off I found some brown ash and began to look for signpost rubs. All I managed to find were a few old rubs from years past. I continued up the brook without finding any sign. After a while, I turned up the ridge and worked my way along it until I found a saddle going through it. I couldn't believe that there was not a sign of any deer being there in the fall. I circled the ridge for about a mile and then worked my way back in the direction of the truck. I finally found a fresh deer track passing through the area when I got to an old chopping. By the time I got back to the truck, after walking for miles, I had only found two piles of droppings that were made the previous fall, but I did not find a single rub or scrape. I couldn't believe how devoid of deer this area was, as it had all the makings of good deer country. Needless to say, I crossed it off my list.

Sometimes a day of scouting ends with a buck on the pole, like the sandwich buck in my first book. Other times, scouting has led me to my next best place to hunt. Scouting days are critical in the big woods, as things constantly change. What was a favorite hunting spot one year may be a clear-cut the next. I've had some of my hunting areas go from good to bad and back to good again over the years. To be consistently successful in the big woods, a hunter is going to have to be willing to do the scouting.

STILL HUNTING

Still hunting is, by definition, moving through the woods slowly and quietly, stopping often to look and listen in hopes of seeing a buck before he sees you. When still hunting, you are trying to find a buck whether he is moving around or bedded down. This is what I call "two points connecting." To be a successful still hunter, the most important thing you can do is to keep yourself in the areas where a buck is most likely to be. A buck spends most of his time in 20 percent of his territory, so that's where hunters should spend most of their time. Too many hunters spend their day wandering around in the other 80 percent of the territory. It's a game of odds, and the more time you spend where there's buck sign, the better your odds of seeing one.

Unlike the scouting days, when the odds of a buck moving around are low, the best still hunting days are when the buck activity is greater. My favorite time to still hunt is on a cool, damp, overcast day. If there is a light drizzle, it makes it all the better. On these kinds of days, buck activity is usually good and it's much easier for a hunter to see and hear everything in the woods.

Another good time to still hunt is on cold, breezy days. On this type of day you have to really use your eyes, as the wind rustling the tree will drown out most other noises. The good news on these days is that all of a buck's senses are dulled, so he will have a more difficult time detecting you. On these days it becomes a game of who sees who first.

My speed as I move through the woods depends on the amount of sign I'm seeing and how far I am able to see. If I can see long ways off, I will move farther between stops. If the woods are thick, I may only take a step or two at a time and spend more time looking and listening. It's more of a feel for the area I'm hunting than anything else. No matter what overall speed I

The author will mark a good signpost like this on his GPS for future reference.

go, my moves are always slow and deliberate, as if I'm in slow motion. Quick movements in the woods are sure to be spotted by a buck.

When I stop, I always try to be against a tree or some kind of cover. The worst feeling in the world is to be standing in the open and hear or see a buck, and not be able to move. I may stop and sit for a few minutes at a time, especially when I see or hear a deer. I may also try some calling if the situation seems promising.

One time while still hunting with a client on a rainy day, we had worked our way into an area I had found while scouting before the season. There were more scrapes in the area than there had been the previous week, so we decided to have a sandwich and try rattling. I looked around for a good place to sit, and although there was no place where we could see in all directions, I finally found a spot that let us

Hal and his son, Gary, with Gary's first Ontario buck, a 205-lb. six-point.

each watch in opposite directions. We sat down, I did some rattling and began eating a sandwich. About 10 minutes had passed when I heard the telltale thump of hooves 30 yards in front of me. A buck had winded us as he came in through the thick brush. The moral of the story is; if you're going to do some calling, make sure you can see all around!

When I still hunt, I spend most of my time hunting the signpost areas, scrape lines and travel corridors. I may hunt the same area day after day, knowing that eventually the law of averages will catch up to me.

One of my favorite signpost areas is in a transition zone between a huge swamp and a hardwood ridge. A lot of brown ash grows along this transition zone and there are two signpost areas about a quarter of a mile apart, where the bucks travel between the swamp and ridges. There have been bucks using these signposts for as long as I can remember. For this reason it is one of my favorite still hunting areas.

One day while still hunting the area with a client, we had made it to the first signpost in time for a 10:00 sandwich. We stayed there for about half an hour and then continued on to the next one. This next area is about 50 yards square, with half of the trees being brown ash. Almost every one of the trees has been rubbed by a buck over the years, and five or six of them are signposts.

On a small knoll above the area there is an annual scrape. It was the first time that I had been there that year, so I stopped to check and see if the scrape had been used. It was torn up pretty good, so I suggested we sit for a while and watch the signposts down in the bottom. Just then I heard a crack and saw a tail waving goodbye in the bottom where the signposts were. I knew it must have been a buck, so we sat down and tried some calling. After a half hour without getting any response, we went down to check where the deer had been. Where the buck had been standing, I could see fresh shavings on the ground at the base of a brown ash tree. He had been making a rub.

Another time while still hunting with Sue Morse, who had been my client for over 10 years, I was showing her some signposts that I had recently found on a a cool, overcast day. We had been at one signpost at the edge of a swamp on the back of a hardwood ridge, and as we hunted towards the next area, a snow squall blew in on the wind. We got to the next signpost area and the snow stopped as quickly as it began, leaving only a slight covering on the ground. This area was in a spring seep on the side of the ridge. The lower end of the seep was open to the hardwoods, but the upper end was a narrow strip of brown ash jutting into a thicket of green growth. It was perfect place for a buck to feel comfortable at his signpost.

We were looking at all the rubs when a deep snort came from the thicket in front of us. I knew we had been busted, but I snorted back at the buck anyway. When we went over to where the snort had come from, I could see that the buck had run out across the hardwood ridge. He had been on his way to the signposts and had either smelled us or heard us there. Who knows, if we had arrived five minutes later, we may have caught him making a rub.

My friend Steve, who owns the camp we stay at in Ontario, has a unique way of still hunting out there. He scouts until he finds an area with plenty of buck sign. Then he goes into the area early in the morning, sits down and uses his bleat call. If he doesn't get a response in half an hour, he will move about 100 yards and try again. He'll continue to do that until he gets a response. When he hears a buck but can't get a look at him, he will try using his grunt call. Steve will hunt an area very slowly, using a grunt call and a bleat call all day. He's just trying to be another deer in the woods. He says he rarely travels more than half a mile in a day hunting that way. It takes a lot of

Guide Bill Werneke with his 200+ lb. heavy-beamed nine-point.

patience, but I can assure you that it works, as Steve has a wall full of trophy bucks.

Anybody can be a successful still hunter by applying these simple techniques: Be quiet, blend in to your surroundings, look and listen often and, most importantly, hunt where the bucks roam.

BARE-GROUND TRACKING

Tracking on bare ground requires a lot of patience and determination. The conditions also have to be suitable to make it effective. Bare-ground tracking can be thought of as still hunting on a track. In most cases you will not be able to follow the track fast enough to catch up to the buck unless he hasn't traveled very far.

I like to track a buck on bare ground for a number of reasons. Number one is that the buck is going to take me through his territory and I will be able to learn it. Number two is, as long as I'm on a buck's track, there is always a chance of killing him. Most of the time a buck will end up leading you to other deer, whether it's where there are does staying or where his territory overlaps that of another buck. Sometimes I'll only follow a track a short distance, but other times I'll follow one for as far as I am able to.

One morning in Maine I picked up a good buck track that had been made since the rain ended a few hours before. The track was easy to follow as the buck was sinking two or three inches into the wet ground. The buck took me across a stream and into an area that I had never hunted. He went a long ways through an area where there were no other deer tracks. Then he went by a few of his scrapes on the way to a hardwood ridge.

When the buck started up the ridge, I could begin to see other tracks showing up. His track was still fairly easy to follow, though, as he continued up and down several ridges. By afternoon the buck had taken me to an area with so many tracks, it was now becoming difficult to follow his. That's when I decided my best bet would be to still hunt my way back to the truck and learn some more of the area. Tracking that buck on bare ground had brought me to a place I may never have found otherwise.

Definitely, the best time to track on bare ground is after a hard rain that has flattened the leaves and washed out any old tracks that may have been made in the mud or sand. Conditions will be much the same after a snow has melted off and left the ground bare again. Once this happens, any new tracks will be evident by the leaves standing up around the tracks' edges. The trail will be even more evident if the leaves are frozen, as the new tracks will look as though they were punched out with a cookie cutter.

It is much easier to track a buck on bare ground if his track is big and he is heavy enough to sink deeper in the leaves. The most difficult

The day before Bobby Graves shot this buck, he and Hal had tracked a buck on bare ground through the area.

55

time to track a buck is when his track mixes in with other fresh tracks, especially those of other bucks. When that happens, I will either follow the easiest track or begin to still hunt the area instead.

Sometimes the track becomes hard to follow if the buck goes through a swamp or takes a trail where the ground is packed hard. That is when you are going to have to think like a buck to try and figure out the most likely direction he has gone. It may be quite obvious or it may take some trial and error. This becomes the case quite often in places like Ontario, where the bucks tend to follow defined trails more often. In any event, tracking on bare ground is a worthwhile challenge that will help you hone your hunting skills.

Whether it's scouting, still hunting or tracking, bare ground hunting should be part of your strategy to hunt bucks in the big woods wherever you choose to do so.

If you spot a doe, make sure to keep looking for a buck nearby. (Sue Morse photo)

Gear and Gadgets

T he clothing and equipment a hunter uses are ultimately his or her own choice. Hunters figure out what works for them in the area that they hunt. In most cases, though, they are not geared up to hunt in the big woods of the north.

If you're a stand hunter, your choice should be warm and comfortable. You need not be worried about weight or bulk. If, on the other hand, you intend to track or still hunt in the big woods, you must gear up for it properly to have the best chance of success.

After guiding deer hunters for more than 20 years, I've found that there are two mistakes they commonly make: One is that they tend to over dress and the other is that they carry too much equipment. I think the reason so many hunters do this is out of fear of being cold or lost. But both over dressing and overloading will cause a hunter to overheat and become worn out, especially when the terrain gets rough. To be a successful tracker or still hunter in the big woods, proper clothing and gear are essential.

CLOTHING

Wool clothing is by far the hunter's best choice for many reasons. Wool is warm, even when wet, but also breathes well enough to cut down on sweating. Wool pants, shirts and jackets are available in all different weights, enabling a hunter to stay comfortable in any temperature or weather conditions. I've hunted in 50-60 degree temperatures without getting too sweated up. At the other end of the spectrum, one year while hunting in Ontario in early December, the temperature was between -20 and -40 degrees every day. It was brutal, to say the least, but the only difference that made in my clothing was that I added a wool vest over my wool shirt. I stayed in the woods all day; I just didn't stop in one place for very long!

The author always dresses with wool clothing.

Wool is water resistant, but it will also keep you warm when it is wet. I can hunt all day in a drizzle or light rain, and the only parts of me that might get wet are my knees, wrists and around my neck. Pouring rain is another story. I know I'm going to be wet, but at least I'll be warm. Pouring rain will run down the back of your neck, until it eventually makes its way to the butt crack. That's usually when it becomes hard to see the fun.

The weather in the north can change in a matter of minutes. I've seen the temperature drop 20 degrees in as many minutes and the snow blow in on gale wind. This can create a

Good wool clothing is necessary for comfort when it's wet or snowy.

dangerous situation if you are not dressed for it. Cotton or synthetic clothing just will not cut it if you get caught in such weather.

When tracking a buck, you also run the risk of falling in a stream or beaver bog. Wool clothes are the only ones that will allow you to stay on a track if that happens. If I get in the water over my boots, I take a few minutes to get comfortable again. First I rub snow on my pants or any other wet clothing. (The snow will absorb the water like a sponge. Beaver trappers roll their beaver around in the snow to dry them out so the water doesn't freeze on the hair.) Then I pull my boots off and empty the water out. While my boots are draining, I wring out my wool socks. Once that's done, I put my socks and boots back on as quickly as possible and get back on the track. With the water out of my boots, my feet will warm back up as I walk.

When you're pushing through a thicket, branches dragging across wool will not make any noise. Likewise when you're walking through the brush, the whips will only make a dull thud instead of a loud crack when they slap against your pant legs. Having silent clothing is critical when sneaking along in heavy cover or putting the death creep on a bedded buck.

I wear a pair of light wool pants until the cold weather and snow comes, then I switch to my heavyweight pants. I wear suspenders to keep the weight off my waist; a pair of heavyweight wool pants really becomes heavy after a day in the rain or snow. Most of the time, I wear a lightweight wool shirt, with a wool jackshirt over it (A Jackshirt has an extra layer of wool on the shoulder area to help shed the rain and snow.) Once the temperature drops near zero, I switch to a heavyweight wool shirt, with the jackshirt over that.

I like the design of the jackshirt. It has a double layer of wool, front and back on the top third or shoulder area, which helps to shed rain and snow without making the jacket too heavy. If it's unseasonably warm, I wear only a shirt. Every person's body regulates differently and it's up to them to figure out the best combination of clothing through trial and error. There are many companies that manufacture wool clothing, but L.L. Bean, Johnson Outdoors and Filson have been my favorites over the years.

For tracking, I would suggest dressing on the light side to start. Underneath my wools, I wear lightweight long underwear, top and bottom. If you tend to perspire, you probably want to wear a wicking type of underwear and stay away from the cotton ones.

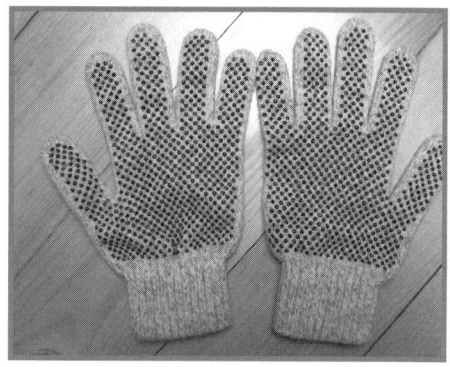

I wear a light hat until the temperature drops to near zero. Then I wear a warmer one with ear flaps for extra protection. Body heat escapes through

Wool gloves are light and warm, and the rubber dots grip your gun.

your head, so wearing a light hat in all but extreme cold helps keep me from sweating. I can also keep my body temperature regulated through my hands. I do this by taking my gloves off when I get overheated. When I'm tracking a buck, it's not uncommon for me to have my gloves on and off every half hour. The colder it is, the quicker I cool down. I wear wool knit gloves with rubber dot grips on them. I've been wearing them since they came out over 20 years ago and have not found anything better for tracking. They fit snug, enabling me to hit the safety and shoot without hesitation. I carry an extra pair in my pack, as it's nice to have dry gloves for a long, cold walk back to the truck.

FOOTWEAR

Your boots are one of your most important articles of clothing for tracking. If you don't have comfortable boots, you are probably not going to be able to put on the miles after a buck. Tracking boots have to be lightweight as well as waterproof. If you have boots that weigh three pounds apiece, you're going to know it after you crawl over blow downs for a few miles. You're also going to struggle if you have wet feet all day.

I like the Lacrosse 18-inch Grange rubber boots. To me they are like wearing sneakers, which is important when trying to sneak around quietly. They are lightweight and the 18-inch height allows me to navigate quite a bit of water without having any going over the top.

Another good choice for hunters who don't like rubber boots is the Maine hunting shoe that L.L. Bean makes, which has a rubber bottom with leather upper. They come in different heights, but I would suggest getting them a least 16 inches high. The leather top breathes better than rubber, but you have to keep them waterproofed with leather dressing.

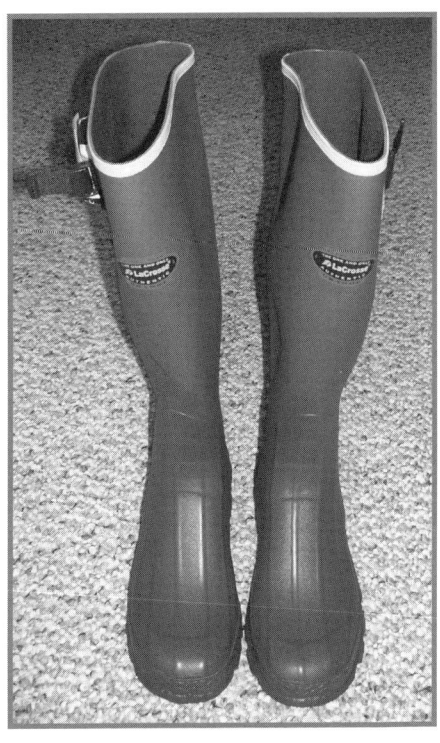

Rubber boots are comfortable and light for long days on a track.

Stiff-soled type boots may be comfortable to walk in, but it is very difficult to feel sticks underfoot. You may end up snapping a stick just when getting in close to a buck. The other drawback to these types of boots is that they are generally not high enough to keep your feet dry when trying to cross a stream. If it takes you 10 minutes to find a place to cross, that's 10 minutes a buck has gained on you.

No matter what you wear for boots, it is equally important to have the right type and combination of socks. The combination that I've found works best for me is wearing one pair of heavy wool socks with a thin polyester sock liner. I wear a boot size that fits snug over this combination, so my feet don't slip inside my boots. Wearing more than one pair of wool socks is not necessary when tracking, as your feet are more likely to sweat than they are to get cold.

PACKS AND THINGS

Having a pack to carry all your essentials is vital. It is also vital that you have the right type of pack for tracking. I think a belt pack is the best choice for many reasons. Number one is that when you're tracking a buck, you'll end up pushing through thickets and ducking under blow downs. If you wear a backpack, it will invariably catch on branches and snap them.

It's getting difficult to find a good quiet belt pack for tracking. I use a medium-sized belt pack made from quiet material, with no straps or buckles to catch in the brush. It's important to have a pack big enough for the essentials but not so big that it's awkward to carry. The best ones I've found are made by Johnson Wool. They are quiet–a basic pouch design with no extra features.

I have certain items that stay in my pack all of the time. These items are in there in case of any emergency, but some have other uses.

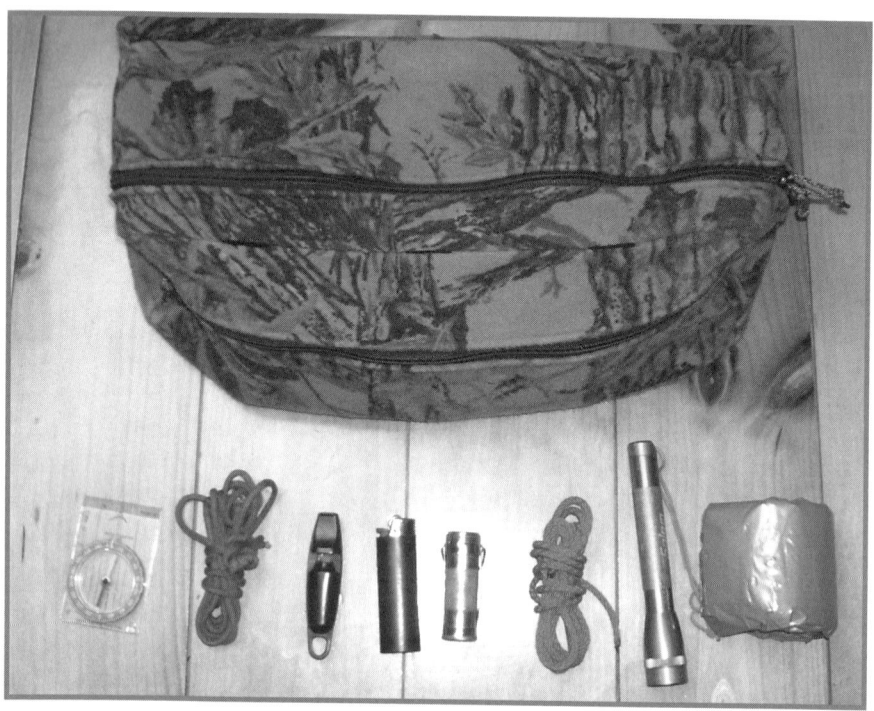

Go light but take some essential equipment.

All together they weigh less than a pound and I think it's well worth the effort of carrying them. These items are:

1) Emergency space blanket (for an overnight stay or temporary rain shelter)

2) Extra compass

3) Butane lighter and waterproof matches

4) Pealess whistle

5) Six-foot parachute cord

6) 10-foot, one-quarter-inch nylon dragging rope

7) Two disposable hand warmers

8) Two chocolate bars

There are some other things that I carry in my pack, and I may change them according to the season or weather conditions. During the rifle season, I always carry an extra clip for my rifle. During muzzle-loader season I carry my possibles bag. If it's rainy or snowy I carry an extra pair of gloves. I also always carry a digital camera and extra batteries. It's important to take pictures of your buck soon after he is down. That is when it will be the easiest to get him into a pose. It's also important to take photos before field dressing, as there will be less blood. If you wait until you get your buck out of the woods, he will have stiffened up and his hair will be flat. These pictures will be the lasting memories of the hunt. Take the time to make them right. With a digital camera I can see how the pictures look immediately. I also carry my camera so I can take pictures along the way. I never know what I might find while in the woods. My camera and gloves go in ziptop bags to keep them from getting damp.

My pack is not complete without my lunch. It's pretty hard to catch up to a buck without fueling up the engine!

There are a few other things that I carry outside of my pack. I have my grunt call around my neck. I carry my snort call in my pants pocket, where I can get at it quickly. I carry my knife on my belt and I usually have some scent in my jacket pocket.

NAVIGATION

The reason very few hunters are trackers is that most hunters have a fear of getting lost. Some hunters have a natural sense of direction, while others are turned around before they get a quarter of a mile from the road. To some of the hunters I know, being able to get out of the woods is as simple as knowing north, south, east, and west. These hunters are as comfortable in the woods as they are at home. Others I know are never going to hunt all that far from a road.

I guarantee that until a hunter gets comfortable enough in the woods so he's not thinking about getting lost, he will never be able to be a big woods tracker. A tracker's mind has to be clear of all things except that buck ahead of him. Somehow God blessed me with that natural sense of direction. I've had it ever since I was a kid. Back then I would wander in the

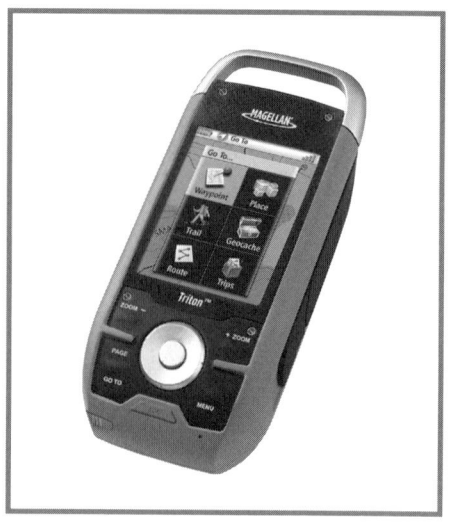

A GPS is handy to mark locations, but, for me, it is not a substitute for a compass.

woods all day without even considering that I might get lost. To this day, I rarely use my compass unless I'm in a snowstorm or in the fog. Those are the two times that it's easy to walk in a circle, and believe me, I've done it. Another time I check my compass is if a buck takes me across a road. This will give me a reference point when the time comes to get out of the woods.

By being able to read a map and compass, anyone can get comfortable in the woods. Every piece of woods is bordered by roads or streams. By looking at a map of the area you are going to hunt, you can find out how big it is. If you know how to read a compass, you can walk a straight line and get out of any piece of woods in a given amount of time. It's a good idea to carry a topo map of the area you're going to hunt. The map will help you get familiar with the area and may also help you to find a shorter way out of the woods at the end of the day.

A GPS is a good tool help a hunter in the woods. There are many makes and models on the market, from the basic ones that allow you put enter in waypoint, to the ones that have map capabilities and will mark your route. I carry a GPS and have found it to be handy for marking points such as signpost rubs or other buck sign. I also use it to mark the position of the truck, if I'm in unfamiliar territory. I've found that part of it is handy for figuring my time to get back out.

Once I mark the truck, I turn the GPS off until I decide to mark a point or check my distance back. Playing with the GPS is not going to help me kill that buck in front of me. I still always check my compass before heading into the woods when in unfamiliar territory. The GPS is an electronic piece of equipment and therefore can fail. Being able to navigate the woods with map and compass is what will really make a hunter more comfortable in the woods.

BINOCULARS

I never go into the woods without binoculars. I don't know how many times they have made the difference in me seeing a deer or not. Years ago, before I used binoculars, I would stare at a brown object that looked like a deer's head or back until I became convinced it had moved. Usually my eyes were playing tricks on me, but once in a while it would turn out to be a deer. Then the problem was trying to figure out whether or not it was a buck, and one I wanted to shoot.

The last straw for me hunting without binoculars was one day when I was tracking a big buck that was with a doe. I had jumped them out of their beds and was following as they made their way up a mountain. I came out of the green growth and into the hardwoods, and I spotted them standing there. The woods were open and the deer were well over 100 yards away. I could see the whole body on both of them, but as luck would have it, I couldn't see either of their heads. The bigger of the two deer was standing a little closer to me, but I wasn't sure if that's why it looked bigger. It was one of those times when I was 90 percent sure it was the buck and I had a good shot, but just couldn't take the chance. After what seemed like an eternity, they both stepped ahead and were gone. Just as I had suspected, the closer one was the buck.

That was the last day of the season for that year and I vowed I'd have a pair of binoculars before the next season rolled around. Now when something looks out of place, I can take a quick check with the binos.

It seems like as my eyes get older I use my binoculars more and more. This is especially true in Ontario, where the swales and clear-cuts offer the chance to glass a lot of country. Another use I've found for the binos is to follow a buck's track. If the buck I'm tracking breaks out into an opening, whether it's hardwoods or a clear-cut, I will stop before following him out into it. I use my binoculars to follow his track across the opening in hopes of figuring out where he might have gone. It's a common trick for a buck to cross an opening and wait on the other side to see if something is following him. If I can see his track turning up a ridge, I'll back up and go above it where I can use the cover.

I like the bra or harness system to carry my binoculars, instead of a neck strap. I find it much more comfortable having the weight dispersed on my shoulders than all of it on my neck. I carry my binoculars under my jackshirt, where the lenses stay clean and dry for the most part. The biggest drawback I've found with binoculars when tracking is that they can get fogged up on the damp days. I recently found an answer to that problem. It's a neoprene cover with a strap to hold it in

A quality pair of binoculars can make a big difference when you're trying to pick out antlers in the brush.

place. It's called an Optic Belt and is a really slick piece of gear.

WOODS GUNS

The only real criteria for a woods gun is that it should be light and fast, with a caliber sufficient enough to shoot through the brush and get the job done. When you're carrying a gun all day long through whatever obstacles you might encounter, a few extra pounds will mean a lot. The type of action doesn't really matter as long as you can operate it quickly. Sometimes a split second can make the difference between getting a shot and a buck getting away.

There are many fine choices of caliber for a woods gun. The .30 calibers seem to be the most popular, but there are a lot of other good choices. I think the .270 and 7mm calibers should be a minimum choice. I know a statement like that will rub a lot of you deer hunters, but here's the reason why I feel that way. Even though a deer is not hard to kill when hit properly from most any caliber, there are a lot of obstacles to shooting in the big woods. The number one is brush. Most anywhere you hunt in the big woods there has been some kind of logging done over the years. This has created good feed and habitat for deer, but it has also made a lot of underbrush in the woods. The odds of getting a perfect broadside shot at a buck with no obstacles is somewhere between slim and none. Light bullets from small calibers are just not suited for shooting through brush. These northern bucks are bigger bodied and have more bone mass than a typical deer. We owe it to these animals to use a bullet with enough energy to get the job done even when the hit is less than perfect. I'm partial to my Remington 7600 carbine, in .30-06. This gun has served me well over the past 20 years and seems as though it has become an extension of my arms. I've always used the 180 gr. round nose core-lock bullets, and they never fail to get the job done.

Since I started hunting deer with a muzzle loader, a lot of things have evolved with respect to these guns. They have come a long since the days of the Hawken rifle with round balls and percussion caps. Even the first of the inline muzzle loaders were finicky at times. I still have nightmares about all the big bucks that escaped me when I was using one of these guns. I can remember while tracking bucks on a snowy day, I'd be praying my gun would go off if the time came! It

The Remington 7600 carbine .30-06 has served the author well over the years.

was a lot of fun and a real challenge, kind of like getting up to bat with two strikes against you.

With the advent of the 209 ignition system and sabot bullet, my confidence in muzzle loaders for tracking has gone sky high. There are lots of good muzzle loaders on the market to choose from. Mine is a Thompson Center Omega, as it's simple, light, easy to carry, and fits me well.

I use a peep sight on my woods guns. When I first started tracking, I had a scope on my rifle, but found that it was hard to keep clear of rain and snow. I take the apertures out of my peep sights so I'm looking through the threaded hole. This allows more light through and doesn't block out any of the target. If you prefer to use a scope, a low power one is more suited to big woods hunting, where shots are typically less than 50 yards. Another good choice is one of the various lighted reticule sights. The only drawback that I can see to these sights is that they use batteries, which don't hold up well in cold conditions.

Whatever gun you choose to hunt with, the most important thing is that you learn to be effective with it. All the gear that I take into the woods barely weighs 10 pounds, and that includes my gun. Don't get bogged down by carrying unnecessary stuff and you'll find that putting on the miles will be a lot easier to take.

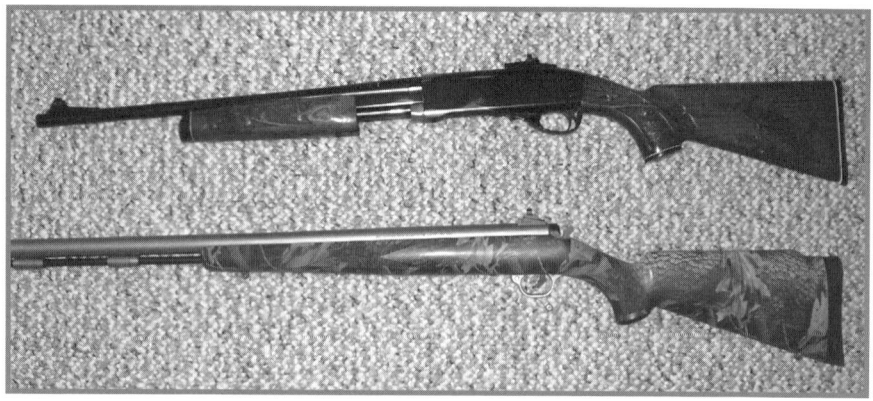

The 7600 carbine (top) and the Thompson Center Omega are the author's favorite big woods guns.

7

The 3 Ps: Practice, Patience, Persistence

No matter how much you read and learn about deer hunting or how many DVDs you've watched, without Practice, Patience and Persistence you will never reach your full potential as a deer hunter. You can spend a lot of time in the woods, but if you are not learning and gaining experience, you are really just out taking a walk.

I can honestly say that I am still working on honing my skills and trying to get better at hunting bucks in the big woods. Every day I'm in the woods, I learn something new and make it a point to apply the

Students surround a signpost rub while attending the author's deer school at Cedar Ridge.

3 Ps. We are all born with a certain amount of natural ability in us; using that, and applying these principles to deer hunting, success is sure to follow. I have to admit, though, that patience is the hardest for me to master.

PRACTICE

To be consistently successful at hunting bucks in the big woods, or anywhere for that matter, it is going to take a lot of practice. Nobody excels at anything without practicing. Tiger Woods didn't pick up a golf club one day and start making 300-yard drives. He practiced seven days a week for years to become one of the best golfers to ever play the game. Likewise, Michael Jordan didn't just pick up a basketball one day and start sinking baskets. He practiced more than most other kids were willing to at the time. Like Tiger Woods, Michael Jordan will go down in history as one of the greatest players in his sport.

Hunting, like any other sport, requires a person to learn and develop certain skills. A lot of these skills can only be honed while you're hunting, but many others can be practiced in the off season. Shooting is one thing that a hunter doesn't want to wait until the hunting season to practice. That would be the same as a basketball player waiting until he got fouled to practice his free throws. Anybody who hunts in the big woods knows that getting a chance at a big buck doesn't come around all that often. So when the chance arises, the hunter better be able to make the most of it.

Shooting practice does not mean going to the range and firing a box of shells at a paper target from a bench rest. Shooting from a bench rest is the proper way to sight in a gun, but once you know that your gun is sighted in, you should practice shooting off hand. The reality of woods shooting is that you will quite often have to take a shot in seconds when the chance arises. Knowing your gun, being comfortable with it and practicing shooting will quite often make the difference in your hanging a buck on the pole.

Clients sometimes ask me what the best gun for them to bring hunting in the big woods would be. My standard answer is usually: the one that they are most comfortable with. If you are going to carry a gun all day, you want it to be fairly light and easy to carry. As I said in Chapter 6, the type of action doesn't really matter as long as the hunter is familiar with it and can operate it quickly.

I learned a lesson about this a while back when guiding a client in a remote camp. We were hunting one day when the wet snow was

If you don't practice your shooting, it could cost you a buck.

piling up in the woods. His was using a pump rifle with a scope that he was very comfortable with. The only problem was that his scope kept filling with snow and fogging up. That night in camp he asked Mike Featherstone if he could borrow his rifle with a peep sight. Mike said sure and the next morning we headed out to look for a track.

Most of the snow had melted, but we found the track we were looking for. After a couple of hours on the track, we caught the buck standing broadside in the hardwoods at about 100 yards. The hunter pulled the gun on the buck and fired. At the sound of the shot the buck just walked off into the brush. I couldn't believe my client had missed a good chance like that, but it turned out to be true. I didn't realize it, but he had never shot a rifle with a peep sight on it. I didn't have a good feeling about him borrowing a gun he was unfamiliar with, but figured that was his own choice. The moral of the story is, be familiar with your weapon and practice with it.

A hunter is far better off to be able to hit a six-inch target in two seconds than to take 30 seconds to hit a one-inch target. I recommend practicing by standing with your gun by your side with the safety on and see how fast you can bring it up and get off a shot. Blow up some balloons to whatever size you want and tack them to a target board. Throw your gun up and shoot one and then bring your gun down and do it again until you are able to hit every balloon quickly. Then throw your gun up and shoot several balloons one after another as fast as you can.

A good way to practice hitting a moving target is to tie full water bottles on strings and swing them from a beam or tree limb. Once again you should throw your gun up and try to hit the bottle as quickly as possible while it is swinging. Practicing like this is more realistic and is also a lot of fun. Just make sure you have a safe backdrop when doing this kind of practice.

The most important thing to practice for hunting in the big woods is walking. If you are going to be a tracker you must be in good physical shape to cover the miles that you might need to. If you don't learn how to walk through the woods, you probably aren't going to get far, and if you do, everything in the woods will know you are there.

The "how" to walk through the woods is actually the most important thing, as it will help you to conserve energy as well as to be silent. By learning where to step you will avoid making noise and have less chance of slipping and falling. Everything in the woods has a noise factor when you step on it. You can practice walking in the woods anytime by trying to sneak up on any animals you might see. When you walk in the woods, you want to blend in and be a part of it. Practice this and it will go a long way towards getting you in close to that buck.

While you're in the woods, you should learn all the different sounds that you hear. Every sound in the woods has a meaning. Learn to identify the sounds: what made them, and why. They are a key to knowing what is going on around you. Sharpen your eyes by picking out the different animals in the woods, whether it's a mouse or a moose. Our eyesight is the one advantage we have over deer, so we have to make the most of it. Many hunters tend to see the woods as a photograph. Learn to see it as a motion picture that you are a part of.

By practicing all of these things you will gain confidence. Confidence is an important component of being a successful hunter. Always be confident and expect that you are going to get your buck. Every day that I'm deer hunting, I expect to shoot a buck. After all, that's why I'm there.

Over my 20-plus years of guiding, I have witnessed a phenomenon that I call "mind-body separation." It happens to bear hunters and moose hunters as well as deer hunters. In deer hunting we might call it "buck fever," which is usually associated with uncontrollable shaking or nervousness at the sight of a buck. Mind-body separation is different in that the person doesn't even suspect anything is going wrong. I've had countless hunters completely miss a bear at 25 yards. Every one of them has told me that he aimed right at the shoulder. At 25 yards, if the bear was in the scope, the hunter would have to hit it somewhere.

I watched a client miss a big buck twice while it was standing broadside at 100 yards. The guy was even sitting down with his rifle resting on his knee. He was convinced that he hit the buck and when we found no sign of the hit, he thought that his scope must be off. We checked his rifle the next morning and it was dead on. Another time I watched a client miss a moose twice at about 100 yards while it was standing quartering towards us. Again, that hunter couldn't believe he had missed.

Perhaps the best example is what happened to one of our clients on a remote hunt. He had been hunting the area for several years and had some favorite spots. One day he was still hunting along a stream when he saw some does cross ahead of him. He decided to wait and see if a buck would come along. Soon, a few more does crossed in the same place, so now he was really excited that a buck might show up.

He didn't have to wait long before a beautiful eight-point buck came along on the trail of the does. He put the crosshair on the buck's shoulder and squeezed off the shot. The buck shuddered at the shot and ran off. Knowing he had hit the buck, the hunter called Mike on his radio, then went over to look for his buck. Mike said when got to the stream the hunter was on the other side and he could see an antler in his hand. The hunter said he had found a shed antler, but Mike knew better. He told the hunter to stop and look at the antler. When he did he realized that he had shot an antler off the buck. Somewhere along the line this hunter's mind saw the crosshair on the buck's shoulder but his body aimed at the antlers.

How can things like that happen when a person seems calm and in control? The only way I can explain it is that the person's body becomes separated from his mind. The mind thinks it's giving the right commands, but obviously the body is doing its own thing. In some cases I believe this occurs from the excitement of the moment, but I think in most cases it occurs from lack of practice, experience or both.

As I said, most hunters tend to practice shooting at a paper target. Then, when they get presented with a shot at an animal they may have never seen, or one bigger than they've ever seen, their mind goes into warp speed trying to figure out what to do. My guess is that they end up pulling the trigger somewhere between calculations and the result is a miss. The biggest common denominator of all the mishaps that I've witnessed is taking too much time to shoot. The longer it takes to shoot, the more time there is to for thought to race through your mind.

Maybe you've experienced a mind-body separation. If you have, I think you'll find that practicing to shoot quickly and knowing where to aim will help prevent you from having another one.

PATIENCE

We've all heard the saying "patience is a virtue." Well, I don't know if that could be any more true than when buck hunting in the big woods. As I said before, patience has been the most difficult thing for me to apply to deer hunting, or anything else for that matter! It drives Deb crazy that I won't wait in line to eat at a

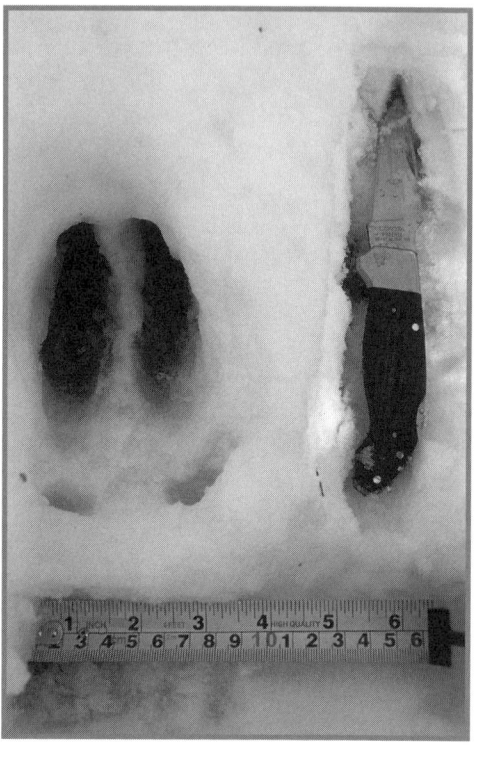

A buck track well worth following! (Sue Morse photo)

restaurant, or that I'll cross five lanes of vehicles to get in the shortest line at a toll booth. I've always been one to try and make things happen instead of waiting for them to happen, but now that I have a granddaughter, I think I'm finally starting to develop a little patience. I know one thing for sure, and that's if I had had more patience over the years, there would be twice as many bucks hanging on my walls.

I have the utmost respect for the hunter who can get in his stand and stay there day after day, without seeing a deer, in hopes that the buck of his dreams will come wandering by. If you're going to stand hunt in the big woods, having patience will overcome the lack of any other abilities you might have. If you have the patience to stay on stand or still hunt in good deer sign, your odds of killing a buck are better than average.

A willow signpost like this is the most common kind in Ontario.

Spruce is a common tree for a buck to rub in the Big Woods. (Sue Morse photo)

A frustrated buck hooked on this willow brush. The bright green color indicates that the buck hasn't been gone very long.

These brown ash rubs were probably made by the same buck at different times. Note the rub on the left has lost the bright color of the fresher one.

Rackasaurus was an impressive sight on the game pole.

This is a traditional rub on a yellow birch.

Here are two images of the same signpost rub on a brown ash. The photo on the left was taken in late October, and as you can see the tree had not been rubbed. The photo on the right was taken the same year at the end of November. It had been rubbed all month by several bucks. The bark shavings were an inch deep at the base of it.

This buck was spotted along a skid trail in the big woods. *(Sue Morse photo)*

The author (left) credits one man as responsible for hunters' interest in tracking bucks in the Big Woods: his longtime friend Larry Benoit.

The most important time to have patience when still hunting or tracking is when you get near a deer. It will require a lot of patience to wait out a deer, as they have all the time in the world. After jumping a deer and hearing it blow or catching a glimpse of it, I'm usually temped to go and look at the track to see whether or not it's a buck. But I've found that by having a little patience, I will quite often learn something by staying put.

One morning in Ontario, I was still hunting on snow, trying to find a fresh track. As I came over a knoll, I saw a buck one bound out of sight in front of me. There was a spruce budworm opening in front of me, so I decided to crouch down and grunt. I blew my grunt call a few times and waited. All of a sudden, I heard the telltale sound of a deer coming from behind me. I turned just in time to see another buck run off. Knowing there were two bucks around, I decided to sit down and grunt some more. I moved over and sat on a log with my back against a cedar tree for cover and grunted again.

A deer started blowing below me on the other side of the opening. I grunted again and then heard another deer blow. I didn't really think the deer would come out where I could see them, but decided to wait anyway. Pretty soon I heard something to my left and an eight-pointer stepped out in the opening 30 yards from me. He was staring down towards where the other deer were blowing. I looked down below and saw a doe and two small bucks work their way out into the opening. None of the bucks ended up being one that I wanted and they all finally wandered off. After spooking the two bucks, I thought the gig was up, but having a little patience taught me otherwise.

When tracking, the time when you are going to need the most patience is when you go into the death creep. This tries my patience the most, because I will try and talk myself into thinking that the buck might have heard me or smelled me and spooked. When I first started trying to figure out how to get close to a bedded buck, I would always rush it. I just didn't have the patience to really go slow. I had a lot of painful lessons in those days!

Another time that it takes patience while tracking is when you have to sort out tracks. If you don't have the patience to do it properly, it is going to cost you precious time or you will give up on it. When a buck's track leads you into a jumble of tracks, you're going to have to sort through them. Sometimes the buck's track is on top of the others and is easy enough to follow. Other times his track will be covered with other deer tracks, or he may have zig-zagged through the tracks. When this happens, the quickest way to find your track is to circle all the tracks looking for it to come out. Quite often you will find the same size track going into the circle. It may or may not be the same buck. When this happens, I just mentally take note of all the same size tracks going into and I follow those going out of the circle. Sometimes the ones leaving will be among those going back in. That's OK; eventually you will end up on the right track or find that the buck is still within your circle. It takes a lot of patience to do this and this is where patience and persistence blend together.

PERSISTENCE

A deer hunter must commit to being persistent if he or she is going to consistently tag big bucks. I feel so strongly that this is the key to success that I'm going to really try and get you to understand the importance of it. Without persistence you are leaving a lot to chance or luck.

Webster's defines persistence as: "to refuse to give up, especially in the face of opposition. To continue insistently, to endure, remain." This is the one trait that the successful deer hunters I know all have in common. Whether they are stand hunters, still hunters or trackers, these hunters persist when others would have given up.

There is a lot of opposition to face in the deer woods. It might be the weather, with bitter cold temperatures, wind, rain or snow. It might be that a buck you are tracking crosses a river or goes into a swamp or heads for the top of the mountain. Maybe you're hungry, thirsty or just plain tired. All these things become opposing forces to be reckoned with . . . excuses that most hunters use when they give up. And that is why most hunters are not consistent at tagging a buck.

It's easy to give up or quit. It's not easy to be persistent. It's also not easy to consistently kill good bucks. If you will just grasp the importance of persistence and practice it, I guarantee you will become a more successful deer hunter.

Persistence is giving 100 percent and being satisfied that you did everything you could that day to

Stay in the woods all day, no matter what.

get a chance at a buck. The biggest racked buck I ever guided a client to was taken by a hunter who committed to staying in that stand all day for the week if need be. As it turned out, he shot the buck at 11:00 a.m. the first day. The point is, he committed to doing it after I told him that a guy sat there the week before but came out for lunch in the middle of every day. Several times I've had hunters shoot a buck on Saturday after sitting on the same stand all week.

We have had hunters that stay in our cabins and hunt on their own without a guide. For these hunters I will show them a couple of places on a map where there are deer, to get them started. I'm amazed at how many will tell me they couldn't find any deer sign there. I know why they didn't; they never went into the woods far enough to find it. They go out for a couple of hours and then go back to the truck for coffee, lunch or whatever. They don't have the persistence to keep going until they find some sign. Then they will go to the next piece of woods and do the same thing. They're trying to make it as easy as possible, and therefore their tag will probably go unfilled. You have to keep going. Spend all day in that piece of woods and you just might find the sign that is made by the biggest buck you will ever shoot.

When it comes to tracking, it is going to take persistence and a lot of it to become consistent at tagging bucks. The old mossy-horn bucks of the north didn't get that way for no reason. Some of them live in the nastiest out-of-the-way places and will take you through some of the thickest, roughest terrain to get there. If you don't persist on these bucks, your chances of killing one are slim. Sometimes you have to press along at a fast pace on a track for hours, just to catch up to a buck. The track might take you through a swamp where you have to struggle not to have water go over your boots. Maybe he goes up over a mountain that is so thick on top that you have to crawl on your hands and knees in places to get through it. Maybe the track takes you into a lot of other deer tracks and it takes a while to sort it all out. Are you willing to do those things? That's where persistence really comes in.

I have hunters tell me all the time that while they were tracking a buck they lost his track. To me there is no such thing as losing a track. Sure, you can misplace it, but the track is still there and you can find it if you have the persistence. One of my better bucks, one that I call Fat Horns, I shot after four hours of sorting tracks in a huge fir thicket that he and a doe had used for a playground all night. The area was too big and thick to circle so I figured my best chance at getting him was to stay on his track.

That buck and doe had raced and chased in and out of head-high fir trees covered with snow and I eventually went everywhere they had gone. I missed their tracks where they jumped across a brook in the middle of some other tracks, which cost me some time. Anyway, through process of elimination, I knew I had missed where they came out of the thicket so I made a circle and found the tracks. Five minutes later, I jumped the buck and doe from their beds. An hour after I jumped them, I shot the buck standing in the hardwoods as I peeked over a knoll. It would have been easy to give up on the tracks, as I was soaked through to the skin from all the snow that went down my neck while crawling through the firs. Instead, I have that buck laying in my living room as a full body mount.

If you are persistent enough, have patience and practice shooting, you will get your buck. There is something I have always called two points connecting. If you keep yourself in the deer woods long enough and hunt the buck sign, eventually you will be at the same place at the same time as a buck. A good friend and fellow hunter and guide, Stan Moody, calls it the "law of convergence." It has to happen—as long as you persist!

Walking the winter deer trails can pay off with a shed antler. Tracks can be seen in a wet gravel road just as easily as in the snow.

Mastering the Art of Tracking

Tracking big woods bucks is an art. Hunters who track bucks are like artists and have different styles or approaches to their work. Some throw paint on the canvas as quick as possible. Others painstakingly pay attention to every detail with every stroke of the brush. When artists are done with their work, the end result will either be just a picture or it might be a masterpiece.

Big woods buck trackers also have different approaches to their work. The end result of tracking a buck is always going to be a "picture" or a hunting experience, but some of these pictures will end up being a "masterpiece" or a trophy on the wall. Like the artist who has a closet full of pictures for every masterpiece he creates, the tracker has a memory full of experiences for every trophy on his wall. The key to putting the trophies on the wall is learning from all the experiences. Hopefully, some of my experiences will help you to create your own masterpiece.

FINDING A TRACK

Obviously the first step to tracking a buck is to find a track. Sometimes this is easier said than done, especially if you're looking for the old toe draggers. These big old bucks are generally a small part of the deer population and the most reclusive. They are also the most difficult ones to track and kill.

Most hunters try to find a buck track by driving logging roads. There are areas in the big woods that have been logged extensively and there is a maze of these roads. A buck that lives in an area like this is eventually going to have to cross roads. If you drive enough of these logging roads, the odds are that you will eventually find a buck track. When you find a track in an area like this, circle the section of woods the buck went into by driving the roads around it. The buck may have already passed through that section and crossed another road.

If you are not familiar with the area, it's a good idea to have a map that shows all of the roads. By circling the area and not finding the buck's track coming out, you have an idea how far away he might be. If you don't take the time to circle the area, you might spend hours on a buck track only to find that another hunter is ahead of you on it. I know of hunters who will find a track an hour before daylight and wait there so another hunter doesn't get on it. It's kind of like staking a claim during the gold rush. The problem with doing that is, while you're waiting, the buck might still be traveling and cross another road. That makes the chance of another hunter being ahead of you on the track even greater. The upside of finding a track from the road is that you haven't burnt up any energy before starting on it. The downside is that putting time in on a track, you may have another hunter ahead of you when it crosses a road.

One year in Maine on the last day of the muzzle-loader season, there was finally some snow to track on. That year there had been very little tracking snow, and since it was my only week to hunt without a client, I was itchy to get on a track. Chris was with me to video and it was going to be our last chance this year to get some footage. The snow that fell in the night was mixed with sleet and freezing rain. There was very little around town, so we drove north hoping to find better tracking snow. As we turned onto a logging road that went north, we found out that there were other hunters with the same idea. There were tire tracks going down all of the side roads, so I knew that taking a track in that area would most likely lead to getting "cut off " by another hunter.

I kept driving north until we reached an area where there were no other tire tracks. Then, just ahead, we could see the telltale pock marks in the snow where a deer had crossed the road. Just as we had hoped, it was the track of a good buck. The buck was heading into a big piece of woods between the road and a river. I didn't think he would cross the river and there were no roads in that area, so we decided to take the track.

The snow was quiet and there was a little bit of wind, making it a perfect day to be on the track of a buck. The track led us down into the green growth where the buck had been checking on does. After about a mile, the buck went up a ridge into some hardwood choppings. There, the buck found another buck that was with a doe and began following them. I was excited knowing that the two bucks might distract each other enough to make it easier to get a shot at one.

Not far from where the tracks came together were running tracks crisscrossing from the bucks chasing the doe. I could see more green growth down below, so I figured the deer had gone into it. The wind was blowing in that direction, and we had just starting to circle around when a deer snorted. I knew the deer had most likely winded us. We made a big circle hoping the deer weren't spooked too bad and we could get around them. Half-way around the circle we cut running tracks heading in the direction of the river.

At that time we were in an old grown-up cut, so I decided to keep moving until I figured out where they might be going. It didn't take long to find out that all three of them jumped into the river and swam across. I was amazed that they did, as the river was 50 yards wide with a lot of current. I guess they just didn't like the smell of us! I knew there was a road about a half-a-mile away from the other side of the river and it would be a good place to check for their tracks.

I marked the spot where the deer crossed the river on my GPS so just in case they didn't cross the road, it would be easier to pick up their tracks again. It was a little discouraging knowing we were going to lose a couple of hours getting back to the truck and driving around. But I didn't think that the deer would go too far once they crossed the river. Usually when deer cross a stream or river they feel safe, because that's how they have been able to escape from coyotes.

We finally made our way to the road on the other side of the river. To my surprise, the deer had walked across it at the top of a ridge and continued along the ridge pretty much in a straight line. I kept seeing running tracks coming back towards us and then circling back. The dominant buck had been chasing the other buck. I kept thinking that it was only a matter of time before I would catch them chasing again. After about an hour I began to realize that the doe was heading to a deer yard that was a few miles away. The deer finally crossed another road and I could see fresh tire tracks in it. My heart sank as I stepped into the road and saw that another hunter was following the tracks. It was a long walk back to the truck knowing my season was over.

When there is a fresh blanket of snow on the roads, it's possible to drive along at a pretty good clip and spot tracks, even before daylight. If there is enough snow, though, some of the logging roads are going to be plowed. When they are, snow is thrown off to the sides making it very difficult to see tracks from the road. Tracks are also hard to spot if the snow is wet and vehicles throw snow from their tires off to the side of the road. In either case you will have to drive slowly looking off into the woods for tracks. Even then it's easy to miss them.

The 7600 .30-06 clip is three-and-a-half inches, so this buck is a monster. Note the dewclaw imprints are way outside of the hooves.

One morning Chris and I were driving a road where we had found a good buck track the day before. I knew there were several good bucks in the area and was hoping to find where one had crossed a road. The snow the day before was wet and had made slush on the roads. The vehicle traffic had thrown the slush way off to the sides, making pock marks in the snow everywhere. Not seeing any tracks on that road, we turned onto a less traveled road that circled back to the first.

Just before we completed the circle, we cut a huge buck track crossing the road–one of those tracks that are as big as they get. The buck track was going into the circle, so I figured that he had to be in there somewhere. The circle was about one mile by two miles. We followed the buck up a ridge, where he began to check on some does. I hunted slowly, thinking that I might catch him chasing a doe. Soon the buck turned towards the first road we had driven and I began to get the sinking feeling that he had crossed it. I picked up the pace, and when we got to the road, there was a truck parked at the track and boot tracks in the buck track. We were so anxious to find a track that I was driving too fast to really scan the woods off to the sides of the road. That was another painful lesson on patience for me!

Those are the reasons that I don't really like to hunt in areas with a lot of roads that can be driven on. I much prefer to strike off through the woods looking for a track. This way I'm hunting and learning something about the area. If you spend all your time riding around looking for a track, you really miss out on a lot. Quite often I will walk back in on a winter road or cart road to see if a buck has crossed. These roads are usually easy walking, making it easy to cover a lot of ground in a hurry. Another reason I like to walk is that bucks have learned to avoid the busy roads as much as possible. Time and time again, I've found where a buck has crossed off the end of a road that is driven on by vehicles.

One time I decided to try an area that I found while moose hunting, though I had never deer hunted it. There was a winter road that circled a ridge and connected two logging roads. There had been snow on the ground for a week, and as I was driving in I could see that there had been vehicles in and out of the road all week. I was thinking about turning around and going somewhere else, but decided to go to the end of the road anyway. When I got to the end of the road where the vehicles turned around, there was not one boot track going down the winter road. It was obvious that everyone in this area was a road hunter.

I started walking down the winter road, and before I was out of sight of the truck, I cut a pretty good buck track that had been made in the night. I decided to continue on and look for a bigger track. About 200 yards farther on, I cut a bigger track going in the same direction as the first. From there I could see another track farther down the road. I walked over to that track only to find that it had been made by another good buck. All three of these bucks had crossed the winter road in the night and were heading in the same direction.

If I don't find a track on one of these winter roads, I turn 90 degrees to the road and head into the woods. Depending on the terrain in the area, I usually will make a big square or a circle, looking for a track. I try to follow a ravine or travel along a ridge hoping to find a track crossing over it. I also check any signpost rubs or scrape lines that I know of in the area. If it's during the rut, I will check around every place I know of where there are does. There are very few days that I do not find a good buck to follow by doing this. The days I don't find a track are usually the ones when there is snowstorm or the day right after one. When it's snowing in the morning, all the hunters in camp get as excited as kids in a candy store, but I know from experience that the odds of finding a track that day are not real good. The reality is that you are going to have to find where a buck has been within a couple of hours or his track will be covered. Once in a while I happen to find such a track, but more often than not I spend a long day searching.

I remember one snowy morning walking back in on an old winter road with a client, hoping to find a toe dragger to follow. There were a couple of inches of snow on the ground and it was coming down steady. About a mile down the road, four deer had just crossed. I suspected one was a small buck and they were heading toward some signposts, so we followed the tracks. We caught up to the does and watched them run off. The buck had split off from them and went to the signposts. There were no big tracks there, so we worked our way along a swamp and back to the road. Just as we got back on the road again, there was another small buck track wandering up it. We followed the track around a corner and a little crotch horn buck was standing there, looking at us. We watched him until he got bored of us and wandered off into the snowy woods. I was beginning to think that it was going to be one of those days when the deer would be moving around everywhere. As it turned out, that wasn't going to be the case. We walked the rest of the day for mile after mile and only found a few other tracks that were made by small deer. As the snow piled up the deer had just hunkered down to wait out the storm.

Guide Mike Stevens was lucky to find this buck's track during a snowstorm, but he was glad he did.

PICKING THE TRACK YOU WANT TO FOLLOW

When I look at a deer track, there are three things that I want to determine. They are the size of the deer, whether it is a buck or doe, and when the track was made. These things determine whether or not it's a track that I want to go follow. Sometimes this task can be quite simple by just glancing at the track, but other times it may require following the track for a while to determine these things.

The first thing I look at is the size and shape of the track itself. Keep in mind that when a deer is walking, the rear foot is placed directly into the front foot print, so the track you see is the rear foot. Keep in mind also that the rear foot is smaller than the front foot. If the track is two-and-one-half inches wide and three inches long, and the dewclaws are a half-inch outside of the hooves, it is most likely a mature buck.

I personally like tracks that are three inches wide, as they are usually made by the old monster bucks. I don't recommend that all hunters hold out for what I call a "3x3 track" (three inches wide and three inches long), since in most places these tracks are few and far between. As I noted earlier, bucks from different areas may have smaller feet. Make sure you know what is realistic for the size of a foot on the bucks in the area you are hunting. The biggest buck that I have taken so far, which you will read about later in the book, is a good example of that. When I saw the track, I almost decided not to follow it even though I had just jumped the buck. If I had been hunting in Maine I wouldn't have, but I knew that in Ontario not all of the big bucks have big feet.

These Ontario bucks' hooves are the same size, but the one on the left is from an older 200+ lb. buck and the one on the right is from a yearling. Note the tips are worn on the older buck's toes.

The shape of a track can help you determine whether or not it was made by a mature buck. As a buck gets older his feet will tend to splay out. This will cause the dewclaws to show more, even in a minimal amount of snow. A mature buck will have dewclaws that show one to two inches behind his toes and they will be noticeably wider than the rest of the track. A mature buck's toes will be rounded or blunt in the front from wear over the years. The print of an older buck will appear to be square because as his feet splay, it causes the toes to spread apart. This square shape will be apparent no matter how deep the snow may be.

The next thing I look at is the length of the stride. I like to see the distance between steps to be 24-36 inches. This measurement can vary depending on how fast a buck is walking. Generally speaking, the longer a buck's stride, the longer his body is, which is a good indication of how much the buck might weigh. Long-bodied bucks will typically weigh much more than short-bodied ones.

The other thing I consider while I'm looking at the stride is what I call the stance–the distance side to side between the tracks. On a mature buck this distance will be 8-12 inches. This measurement is an indication of how wide a buck's body is, and another hint of how much he might weigh.

The last thing I look for is if the buck drags his feet in the snow. Mature bucks have a tendency to drag their feet, and the older they get, the more they drag them. I call them the cross-country skiers. These bucks drag their feet so much that the when you see the tracks, it looks like someone was skiing through the woods. I can assure you that I never walk past one of those tracks!

Quite often I am asked if there is way to tell a buck track from that of a doe. The answer is that there is no foolproof way to tell by just looking at the track. That's why we have to combine looking at the track itself and then considering the other indictors like the ones I mentioned previously. That being said, there are still some mature old does in the woods that have big feet. Some of them will even display dewclaws that look like a buck's. These are usually barren does that have no fawns and are alone. This is another reason you may confuse their track with that of a buck. There is also no way to tell a yearling buck track from that of a doe, as the bucks dewclaws have not yet matured. Anyone who thinks he can tell a buck track from a doe track 100 percent of the time has probably not tracked a lot of deer. I have tracked literally thousands of deer in my life, and I'm here to tell you that I will get tripped up once in a while.

Sometimes you may just have to follow the track for ways to determine whether or not it was made by a buck. It shouldn't take you long to figure it out and it might just be worth the time. I rarely go more than several hundred yards on a track before I determine whether or not it was made by a doe. A doe acts totally differently than a buck and there are several things that I will be on the lookout for. If the track is wandering and feeding, especially within sight of a road, it is probably a doe. If the deer goes between trees that are too close together for antlers, it's probably a doe. The one way you will be able to tell absolutely for sure if you're tracking a buck or doe is when they urinate. When a doe urinates, she squats down like a female dog. This will be obvious in the snow, as the back feet will be spread apart and pointed out. The urine spot will be a small round hole in the center of the tracks. When a buck urinates, he stands with his hocks together and the urine will be in an oblong hole and splattered. Then there will most likely be drops of urine in the snow along his trail as he continued walking.

Not all that long ago I followed what turned out to be the biggest doe track that I have ever seen. I picked the track up where it crossed the road in the middle of the day. That morning I had been tracking a buck that had crossed the border and I had to leave it. The conditions were near perfect with wet snow, and I was anxious to get on another buck. This track was a 3x3, with huge dewclaws, so I assumed it must be a buck. I had only gone 50 yards on the track when I started having my doubts.

The deer had started feeding within sight of the road. I still didn't believe it could be a doe with a track that big, so I continued on it. Within 100 yards, the track turned towards a green knoll, so I thought the deer was most likely lying down. I circled up onto the knoll and found a bed with a track walking away from it. The deer was feeding again and little did I know that I had already spooked it.

Big does will often have big tracks.

I came to the running track which was headed back towards the road. This deer was not acting like a buck, but I still clung onto hope. I followed the track back across the road and up a ridge for about 100 yards, where the deer had stopped to urinate. There, written in the snow as plain as day, was the spread out tracks and round urine hole of a doe. Needless to say I was disappointed, but at least it had only taken about 15 minutes to find out for sure.

Obviously, if you follow a track that you are unsure of and you come to a rub or scrape, you can make an easy confirmation, but quite often a buck will travel a long way without making any. That's the reason it's much easier to look for doe sign. If there is more than one deer traveling together, there is another way to determine if one of them is a buck. If the bigger track is walking on top of the small track, it is most likely a buck following a doe. If the small tracks are walking on top of the bigger ones, it is most likely a smaller doe or fawn following a doe.

AGING TRACKS

There are two important reasons to be able to tell the age of a track. The first is to decide whether or not to follow a particular track. If I am going to take a track in the morning, I want to make sure that it was made the previous night. If it was, I will catch up with the buck sometime during the day. The later the track was made in the night the better, but it doesn't really matter as long as it's the buck I want to follow.

The second reason to be able to age a track is so that you can sort through a maze of tracks without losing the buck you are following. Once you become good at aging tracks, you are well on your way to mastering the art of tracking. That being said, figuring out how long ago a track was made is the most difficult part of tracking for a hunter to learn. That is because there are so many variables that factor into it. I relate these factors to figuring out a mathematical equation. Basically it a combination of the type of snow, when it last snowed, current temperature and past temperature.

Obviously, if it had snowed in the night, it is going to be quite simple to guess the age of a track. All you really need to know is when the snow stopped and how frozen the print is. Once the snow has been on the ground for a few days, it becomes critical to know the difference between a track that was made the previous night and one that is two days old. I've heard countless stories by hunters who said they lost a buck track when it got mixed in with other tracks. If those hunters were able to age the tracks, it would have helped them to stay on their bucks.

When a track is made in the snow, the conditions begin to affect it almost immediately. This is where the calculations come into play, and once you learn them it becomes second nature. I look at track in two separate ways: the bottom of the print and the top edge of the snow. Sometimes one will tell me more than the other, but by looking at both of these things I can age a track to within 15 minutes if the conditions are right. A track is either freezing or thawing, depending on the temperature, but in either case it is changing. The only exception is when the temperature is within a few degrees of the freezing point, in which case a track will stay the same for a long period of time.

When I look at the top edge of the track, I'm looking to see how crisp and sharp it is and also how crisp the snow is that was pushed up in front of the track. This edge changes very quickly and is the single most important thing to look for when sorting through tracks. I was tracking a buck with my son Gary one day when I had the opportunity to teach him this valuable lesson.

We had picked up the track from a road just after daylight that morning. Within half an hour we had jumped the buck. The buck took us up on a ridge where there were other deer. Our buck started to walk in the tracks of another buck with the exact same-size track. That other buck's track was made in the night, so both looked similar. When I asked Gary if he could tell the difference, he said that they looked the same to him. I pointed out that the track we were following still had a sharp edge and the one made in the night was just slightly rounded on the edges from evaporation in the cold air. The difference was only noticeable to Gary when we got down and looked closely at the track. Sometimes these subtle differences are the only way to keep you on the trail.

When I examine the bottom of the track, I do most of it by feel when it's cold and by sight when it's warm. When it's warm the print itself will melt until, eventually, there is nothing more than a square hole in the snow with bare ground in the bottom. How long this takes depends on the temperature. When it's cold the print freezes, so by feeling how frozen it is I can get an idea of when it was made. Again, the temperature will determine how fast the print freezes.

These examples are best suited to new snow on bare ground. When there are several layers of snow, the print become harder to see, as the snow falls back into the track. Once this happens, I rely more

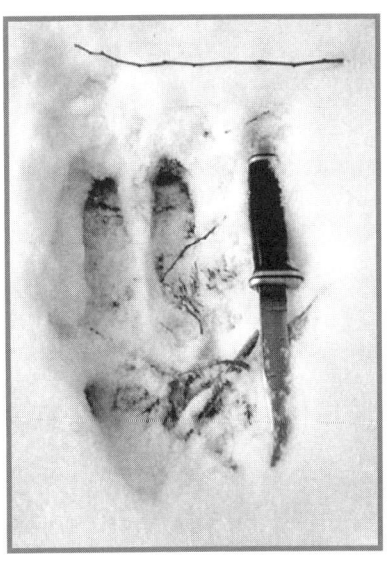

This monster buck track is crisp, clear and fresh.

on looking at the top edge of the track and also feeling its inner edge. The inside edge of the track will get firm or set up when it's cold. This will actually happen quicker than the edge rounding over. Feeling the loose snow on the inside edge of the track is the quickest and easiest way to tell if the track has just been made. Whenever I feel in a track, I always use my bare hand. With gloves on, you just cannot be accurate enough.

The only way to get good at aging tracks is by experience. A good way to get the experience when you can't be in the woods is to make tracks around your property. You can experiment all winter if you live in an area that has snow. It doesn't matter if you make the tracks or your dog makes the tracks; all you need to do is to keep checking on them to see how they change over hours and even days. You can also go out in the woods and track other animals, such as fox or coyote, to get some practice. You'll be surprised at how much you will learn by doing it, and it will give you a head start on your next deer season.

ON THE TRACK

Once I decide to follow a buck's track, I'm going to hunt it two different ways. If the track is hours old, I'm going to hunt the track to catch up to the buck. The odds are that the buck is bedded down somewhere and I want to catch up to him as fast as I can. The quicker I can catch up to a buck, the more time I will have to hunt him.

All too often a hunter will move slowly along on a track that was made in the night and never get close to the buck. It's not uncommon for a buck to travel five or 10 miles in one night. If you find his track where he had just begun to travel, it is going to take you a while to catch up to him. Until a buck gives me some indication that he is lying down or the track begins to get fresher, I am going to move along at a fast walk. By moving fast, most of the time I can catch up to the buck within three or four hours.

If I think a track is less than an hour old, whether I have been following it for a while or I have just found it, I will hunt it at a slower pace. This pace will depend on what the buck is doing. If he is moving along in a straight line, I will still move fairly fast, but I will also be looking more closely at the woods ahead. If the buck is checking does or laying down rubs and scrapes, I will move more slowly, really taking the time to search the woods. I want to try to get look at the buck before he gets a look at me.

Whenever you're on a buck track, you have to become a student and learn from that particular buck. I don't care how many bucks anyone has followed, there is always something to be learned from each one. You may learn where one of his secret hideouts is, or he may take you to one of his signpost rub areas. You may also learn places that other bucks are using. By following a buck, you will also find out where all the does in his area are. All of this information is going to be useful the next time you end up hunting in the same piece of woods.

Bucks are born with certain basic instincts, but most of their behavior is learned over the course of their lifetime. That's why an old mature buck is the most difficult one to kill. A buck's whole life is spent trying to avoid danger, and they become good at it. Once a buck is successful at eluding danger by employing a certain trick, he will most likely use the same trick again. In the big woods, predators like wolves and coyotes have the most influence on a buck's behavior. A buck will use the same tactics to escape when being followed by a hunter as he does with a predator. It's important for a hunter to learn these different tactics, and use them to his advantage.

One of the most common tricks a buck will use is to turn around and walk back in his track for a ways and then jump off to one side. This gives the buck time to gain some ground while whatever is following him is trying to figure out where he went. A coyote is going to follow the track to the end and then it will take him a while to find where the track went. Likewise, a hunter on the track might also take some time to figure out where the buck went. Once the buck you are following uses this trick, you should expect him to use it again. As soon as you see the buck's track coming back towards you, immediately look off to both sides for his jumping track. Every time you can catch the buck using this trick, you will gain some time on him. With any luck, you might even catch him coming back on his track.

Another common trick that bucks use to escape danger is to walk in water. They've learned that by walking in water they can lose a predator. It's quite common to follow a buck to a stream and not see the track come out the other side. When this happens, he buck has obviously walked one way or the other in the stream. First, I always look in the direction the buck was traveling. If the stream is shallow enough, I will walk in it and look for water dripped on rocks or ice to confirm that I'm going in the right direction. All the time that I'm doing this, I'm also looking on both sides of the stream bank for his track. If I come to a log that is lying across the stream or a spot where the ice is frozen across the stream and I do not see any sign, then I know that the buck has probably traveled the opposite way. At this point, I turn around and search the other direction.

I have followed bucks in streams for several hundred yards before they left them. The water doesn't have to be a stream for a buck to walk in it; they will quite often walk the wet places in the woods where the snow has melted and left puddles on the ground. This quite often happens in skidder trails and spring seeps. Once you know a buck is using the water like this, it's much easier to pick his track back up. Just walk in the water and keep looking for the track leaving it. No matter what trick a buck uses to try and lose you, the sooner you can figure it out, the faster you can gain ground on him.

The one escape tactic that some bucks use is to run. I don't mean that the buck runs off a ways and settles back down, but that these bucks might run a mile before stopping. My experience with such bucks has been that they are very wary and never let their guard down. You will never gain ground on a running buck until he decides to stop. Usually these bucks give no indication that they are going to lie down, and they will be watching their back track when they do. Once they see movement following them, they are up and running again, and may travel another mile before stopping again.

When I discover that the buck I'm following is one of these running bucks, I know I'll be putting on some miles that day. I hunt these bucks with two objectives in mind. One is to pressure the buck by moving fast on his track in hopes of catching him looking back just long enough to get a shot. The other objective is to find another good track to switch to. Experience has taught me that my odds of shooting a buck that is not a runner are much greater than shooting one that is. Once you figure out a particular buck's bag of tricks, you just might be able to anticipate his next move.

Just when I thought that I had seen every trick that a buck might use, not long ago a buck showed me a new one. It was the last day of the muzzle-loader season in Maine, and there had not been any tracking snow all season. It had rained in the night, so I hoped that there might be some snow in the higher elevations. As I was driving to the place I wanted to hunt, there started to be a covering of wet snow on the ground. Now I just hoped that I could find a good buck track to follow.

I walked back in on an old winter road to look for tracks. About a mile back in the road was blocked with alders, and I went into the woods to get around them. I knew there was a stream not too far ahead, so I decided to walk to it and follow it back to the road. As I was walking along the stream, I stumbled across a signpost rub. It was a nice-looking one, and I decided to stop and take a photo of it. I was kneeling down taking the photo when I noticed the slight dimple of a buck track beside the tree the rub was on. There was only an inch of snow on the ground, and I was wondering if the track might just be an old one in the mud under the snow.

As I carefully scraped the snow out of the track with my finger, I could see that the bottom of the track had packed snow in it. That confirmed to me that the track had been made in the night. I put away my camera and headed out after the buck. Since it was still snowing lightly, I moved quickly on the track not knowing if I could catch up to the buck before the track became totally filled in with snow.

The buck crossed the stream and hadn't gone far when he found some does to check on. There had also been another buck checking those does, and that buck's track was fresher. I took the fresher track and hurried along on it before it filled in with snow. After following the buck for four hours, I knew he must be still up and moving, as the amount of snow in the track didn't change. The buck was still wandering and searching for does, stopping once in a while to make a hooking. He buck took me to an area that I was familiar with, just as his track was beginning to get fresher. I started to creep along, thinking I would see the buck at any minute. The conditions couldn't have been more perfect for killing him.

The buck walked over to a blown-down spruce and fed on the old man's beard on both sides of it. There was now no snow in the track, so I knew I had missed the buck feeding there by minutes. I continued easing along on the track as it crossed a swale and disappeared into the cedars on the other side. I knew the buck was looking for a place to bed down and I was going to have to try and catch him in his bed. The buck left the cedars and crossed the same swale farther down and went into the dark spruce.

Just inside the spruce I could see where the buck had been standing and then had jumped back to the left. I looked up the swale and thought that the buck might have seen me when I crossed it, following his track. I was bummed out and decided to wait a half hour for him to settle down. The wind was blowing into the woods from the swale, so I decided to move into the spruce and find a log to sit on. I had eased down the buck's track a few jumps when I spotted a round brown patch of fur 30 yards in front of me.

I knew it was the buck, but couldn't tell what part of him I was looking at. There were spruce limbs everywhere, and as hard as tried, I could not make out any part of the buck. I took a step to the left and then one to the right, but still couldn't make anything out. All of a sudden, I saw a thick dark rack with tall tines move back and forth. Then the buck's shoulder came into view and I knew he was going to bolt. I swung the bead onto his shoulder and fired just as the buck bolted. I knew I had missed as soon as the gun went off. My sight picture was high on the shoulder and the buck dropped down when he bolted.

Needless to say, I was sick! The buck was a heavy-bodied one with the antlers to match. I followed the track for about 50 yards, just to make sure I had not hit the buck. Seeing that I had not, I broke off some fir boughs and sat down on a log to wait. I sat there thinking about why I hadn't seen any other part of that buck standing there. The brown spot I did see was his hind quarter. He had been standing in his bed looking back over his shoulder at me and his head was up in the spruce limbs. I guess all the limbs and the blowing snow made good camouflage for him.

I couldn't eat a sandwich, but I did manage to get down a cookie. Then I reloaded the speed loader I had used and had just put it back in my pocket when I looked up to see the buck walking back towards me at about 40 yards. He stopped behind some firs where I couldn't see him. I held the gun on the firs thinking he was going to step out. After 10 minutes of waiting, I knew something wasn't right, so I walked over to the fir thicket where I had last seen the buck. He must have caught wind of me, as he had run straight back away from me for a few bounds and started to walk again.

Now I'm thinking that this buck must have a death wish! I followed him for about another half hour, when his track jumped to the left again. I could see a cow moose up ahead and thought maybe the buck was spooked by her. I followed the running track about 50 yards, and there was the buck's bed with a running track leaving the bed, so I knew that I had jumped him again. That was twice that this buck had jumped off to the side of his track and lain down to watch it. I had never seen this before, but now I was onto him.

This time I went right after the buck without waiting, in hopes of catching him before he lay down again. About a half hour later the buck was back to where he had fed on the blow-down. Then, once again, he jumped to the left and headed into a thick patch of spruce. This time I left his track and circled slowly around, looking to see if his track came out. When I closed the circle, I knew the buck was bedded down again. I looked at my watch and it was 3:00. It would be dark in an hour and I was about three miles from the truck. Even thought the buck was close, it would take me an hour or two to hunt that piece of woods and have a chance of killing him. It was a tough decision, but I headed out for the long walk back to the truck.

As soon as I start to follow a track, I'm trying to figure out where that particular buck might be going and what he is doing. Everything a buck does and everywhere he goes is deliberate. I always try to get into the mind of the buck that I'm tracking, so I might be able to determine what he is up to. The time of the season will also help me determine what a buck might be up to. Before the rut, a buck that is traveling pretty much in a straight line, and not stopping, has some-place in his mind where he wants to be. That place could be the next mountain over or it could be a hideout he has five miles away. In most

Dave Delair poses with his 220-lb. eight-point. His guide, Tom Hamilton, was on the track when the buck came by Dave.

cases the buck is already there and bedded down, and the best thing for hunter to do is hunt the track as fast as they can and catch up to him. The sooner you catch up to a bedded buck, the more time you will have to hunt him.

During the rut, a buck will be checking on does most of the time. Typically, these bucks keep moving until they find where a doe has been and then they begin to wander and search for her by scent or by following her track. When a buck is doing that he is not paying as much attention behind him, and it's a good time to catch him off guard. In either case, the sooner you can figure out what a buck is up to, the better the chance you will have at getting a shot at him.

What a buck has been doing is written in the snow by the tracks he leaves. I got the chance to show a classic example of this to one of my clients during the rut not long ago. There were a couple of inches of snow on the ground and the plan for Ed [last name?] and I was to find a good buck track to follow. We left the truck and headed for a cedar chopping where I knew there had been some does living. As we worked our way around the chopping, we found the track that we were looking for.

The buck was following a doe's track up the hardwood ridge above the cedars. The tracks were fairly fresh, so we worked our way up the ridge hoping to catch the buck off guard. We hadn't gone far when we came to the doe's bed, with her running tracks leaving it. I knew then that the buck had caught up to her. I told Ed there was a good chance that we might catch them chasing, so we needed to be watching carefully up ahead.

The buck followed the doe up to a shelf on the ridge and then they began to walk parallel along it. Every once in a while the buck would chase the doe around, and then continue walking in the same direction. I knew they would eventually lie down, but I was hoping we would catch them before they did. The wind started to blow and it began to spit snow, making it a perfect day for tracking. Pretty soon another doe got in with our deer and all three walked up a small knoll. There was a ravine on the other side of the knoll and I thought we might catch them in it.

As we peered over the top we could see a deer standing on the ridge across the ravine. When I looked with my binoculars, I could see that the deer was a spike horn. I could also see the tracks we were following had gone past the spike horn and over the ridge. Now we were going to have to get around the spike horn without spooking him or have him spook the other deer. The spike started to feed his way down the ridge, so we just waited for him to get out of sight.

Waiting on the spike horn had cost us about 10 minutes, so we picked up the pace a little. The deer made their way into a hardwood chopping where two more tracks joined in with them. One was a doe and the other was another good buck. Things were starting to get exciting, but the problem we had now was that there were 10 eyeballs to see us. All five tracks stayed in line as they went back down the ridge through the chopping. It was really windy out in the open, and I assumed the deer were going down out of the chopping to bed down.

The deer went across a small clear-cut with a green knob on the other side. The knob was cleared except for a few patches of small firs, so I didn't think the deer would stay out there in the wind. There was also no way to circle around the knoll, as it was open all around it. We followed the tracks to the knob where they started to go up, then turned and went around the side of it. The deer had slowed down and were starting to wander, and I was starting to get that "gut feeling" like something was going to happen.

We were easing slowly along the right side of the knob with thick firs on our left. The tracks were heading down towards another ravine, so I focused out ahead of us, hoping to catch a glimpse of brown. We had moved ahead a ways before I glanced down at the tracks again. When I did, I noticed that the tracks had turned left into the firs. At that instant I knew the deer were right there on the knoll. Too late, just as I looked to the left I could see a doe and a heavy-horned buck sail off the knoll only 30 yards from us. Ed had seen them at the same time and he ran ahead to try and get a shot. When he did, two more does jumped up in front of him and ran down into the ravine. By the time we ran to the other side of the knoll, the buck had disappeared down off the ridge.

I knew Ed was disappointed at not getting a crack at that beautiful buck. My emotions were somewhere between disappointment and disgust with myself for not going with my gut feeling and stopping to think over the situation. When looking things over, we could see that the deer had a good place to bed out of the wind in the firs on the back of that knoll. If I had paid more attention to the tracks, I would have seen them turn into the firs. It would have given us a chance to circle back around and get above the deer. It's times like that when an old buck will keep you humble.

Not long ago I read an article that talked about gut feelings and explained what they are. Everybody gets them and for all kinds of reasons. The article said that all of our experiences are stored away in our subconscious minds. A gut feeling arises when our mind pulls together all of our past experiences when we are in similar situations. The article also said that it was a good idea to trust your gut feelings. I knew when I was following those tracks that the buck was going to stay with the doe and they would eventually bed down. I had just talked myself out of thinking that they would be on that knoll. I always seem to have to learn these lessons the hard way!

THE DEATH CREEP

The two things that hunters have the most trouble with when tracking a buck are sorting out tracks and knowing when and where a buck might be bedded. We covered sorting tracks in Chapter 7, and I wrote about it in my first book as well. I also wrote about getting in close to bedded bucks, but feel I need to expand on the subject in a couple of areas.

Mature bucks are loners, and unless they are with a doe, they will find a secure, out-of-the-way place to bed down by themselves. Just because a buck heads into a swamp, thicket or up a ridge doesn't necessarily mean that he is going to bed down. But if a buck does stop to feed before going to one of these places, there is a good chance that he is going to be bedded. When a buck is traveling, he doesn't usually take the time to feed; he will usually feed when he gets to where he wants to lay down.

When a buck that I'm following starts to wander around and feed, if the terrain allows it I will circle the area the buck is heading into and look for his track coming out the other side. By doing this I don't waste any time. If I find his track coming out of my circle, I just continue on it. If I don't find his track when I circle, I have the buck located and can take all the time I need to hunt for him. If I can get the higher ground when the buck is bedded on a ridge, I will go behind the ridge and get above the buck. Then I still hunt slowly in a zigzag manner, trying to catch the buck bedded or get a shot when he jumps.

Roger Kingsley took his first Big Woods Buck while tracking it with his guide, Rocky Achey. One hundred ninety-six pounds and eight points is a good start.

If the buck goes into a thick area, I know my chances of killing him by staying on his track are much better. I call this the "death creep," and it is the most difficult aspect of tracking to master. Once you close in on a buck and kill him using the death creep, you've accomplished something that very few deer hunters ever will.

The death creep requires the hunter to be alert at all times with eyes and ears. You have to be able to detect the smallest patch of brown that is out of place. You also have to be able to detect the slightest sound of a twig breaking or the dull thud of the buck getting to his feet. Good balance is also crucial to being able to put on a death creep. You will have to be able to stand on one leg until you can get your other foot planted on the ground. All of this is going to require concentration and patience. The death creep is the end game or culmination of all the work you put into catching up to a buck.

When I start my death creep, I take one small step at time. Every step will give me a whole new picture of the woods. Before I take each step I lean forward and scan every inch of the woods in front of me as well as off to both sides. Quite often the buck will walk around a blow down or thicket and watch his track from the side. I also follow the track out as far as I can see it with my eyes to try and figure out where he might be bedded. I play out this whole process as if I were in slow motion, as any quick movements are sure to be spotted by a bedded buck. My entire goal when going into the death creep is to either shoot the buck in his bed or get close enough to him to get a good running shot when he jumps.

The conditions are going to play a big role in the success of a death creep. If it is a still, calm day, it will be a lot harder to get in close to a buck. His hearing is so acute that he will hear the slightest rustle of a branch or twig snap underfoot. The best chance of killing a buck while you are in the death creep is when it is windy, and especially if it blowing snow. These conditions help to cover your sound and your motion. Later in the book you will read about my successful death creep on the Island Buck, but sometimes things don't always turn out as planned.

One morning while hunting out of a remote camp during the muzzle-loader season in Maine, I picked up a good buck track at daylight. It had snowed about six inches in the night and it was still coming down. The track was half filled in with snow, but I knew that it couldn't be more than a few hours old. I had only gone about a quarter of a mile on the track when I came to the buck's bed with no snow in it. At first I thought I had jumped him, but then I saw that his track was

Guide Rocky Achey with a 220-lb. nine-point he shot standing in his bed after a slow death creep.

walking away. I thought to myself, it doesn't get any better than this.

Big snowflakes were coming down and the visibility was only about 50 yards. I had a good feeling this buck was going to be mine. I followed him across a brook and up onto a ridge, all the while thinking that I would see him at any minute. The buck then went around some softwood knolls, as he looked for does. After a while he dropped back down a hardwood ridge and into a ravine. Then a steep ridge appeared in front of me with the buck's track going up it. It was snowing so hard that I hadn't seen the ridge, and now I was afraid he was bedded on top and might have already seen me. There was a ledge going straight up on my right and a ledge dropping off to the left. The buck was moving up a passage way between them. My only choice was to death creep up his track.

I eased up the steep ridge with every step giving me another view over the top. All of a sudden, the buck stood up in front of me at 25 yards as if he were in slow motion. He had been lying behind a log and must have seen the top of my head. As I started to bring my gun up, I couldn't believe he was going to stand there. The muzzle loader I was using was my old Hawken rifle with a Lyman peep sight mounted on the tang. I kept trying to pull the hammer back, until I realized that I was pulling on the sight instead of the hammer. Just as I reached over and pulled the hammer back, the buck bolted. I got lined up on him to shoot, but my feet slipped and by the time I caught myself, the buck had disappeared over the ridge. It's hard to remember all the thoughts that were racing through my mind, but all I knew was that I had just blown my chance at one of the best bucks I'd seen in quite a while. He would have dressed out at well over 200 pounds and had thick, dark beams and tall points.

My mistake was carrying a gun that I hadn't used in years and was not accustomed to. I hadn't realized until the day before the season that I didn't have enough bullets for my Gonic inline, so I'd dug out the old Hawken rifle. The hammer on the Hawken is on the right side and I'm left-handed, making it awkward in the first place. I guess when my thumb felt the peep sight, I subconsciously thought it was the hammer and started pulling on it. I had two more running shots at that buck that day, but didn't connect with either one. Later that week, I missed another good buck with the Hawken and swore I would have a muzzle loader that felt right to me by the next season. Another hard lesson learned.

SANDWICH TIME

The one tactic I use that has help me and my clients kill more bucks while tracking is to wait after jumping a buck. I wrote about this in my first book, and since it was published, this is the one thing that more hunters have told me helped them kill their first buck by tracking than any other. So I feel the subject is important enough to go over again and add to.

Nine times out of 10 when you jump a buck, he will run for a short distance and then stop, waiting to see if anything is going to follow him. He may have only run because he heard a stick break or saw movement, and doesn't really know what it is that spooked him. By going after a buck as soon as you jump him, you will most likely find a spot where he stood looking back at you. The tracks leaving that spot will be running, as he spotted you and knows something is after him, and now the buck will always be watching his backtrack. That makes getting a shot at him a lot harder. I've found that by waiting half an hour, the buck will assume nothing is following him and will settle down.

At first I tried waiting 15 minutes, but found that it was not long enough. I usually have a sandwich while I'm waiting to help pass the time. I also make sure to look at my watch, as waiting for 10 minutes can sometimes seem like an hour. Once I take up the track again, I expect that the buck has done one of two things: He is bedded down again, in which case I'll have to figure out where. Or he started traveling, in which case I am going to have a better chance of catching him moving.

I'd like to clarify a few things about this tactic and when I vary from it. There are basically two times that I will forego the wait. One is when I've waited my half an hour and end up jumping the buck again. If I jump the buck a second time, I probably won't wait another half hour, as the buck now knows something is after him. I'll have to catch him making a mistake. The other time I don't wait is when a buck is with a doe, paying more attention to her than what is behind him. The doe will want to keep an eye out behind her, but the buck will have her distracted, making it much easier to catch them off guard.

Once you learn the basics of tracking, you have to keep applying them until you get results. I always tell hunters that if they keep repeating what they know to do, the law of averages will eventually catch up to them. So get out there and find a track to follow. The journey in tracking is all about the experiences along the way. It might be in the woods you explore or the wildlife you see. Whatever it is, once tracking is in your blood, it will be like a virus you'll have to live with.

Tim Burnell's first Big Woods Buck was shot while tracking a bigger buck with the author.

There are several factors you must take into consideration before you decide to either follow a wounded buck right away or wait. (Sue Morse photo)

Finding a Wounded Deer

In a perfect world, all of us hunters would hit our mark exactly where we aimed and there would be no need to write this chapter. The reality is we are all human beings and therefore will eventually misjudge, goof-up or make a mistake when shooting at a deer. There are also many things out of our control that can result in a poor shot. The deer could move just as you fire your shot or you could hit a tree or branch. I personally would much rather have a clean miss than to wound a deer or any animal. A wounded deer in some areas may heal up and survive, but in the big woods a wounded deer's fate is sealed. If he doesn't die on his own, coyotes or wolves will take over. Either way, there is no good result to not finding a wounded deer. The deer is going to suffer and the hunter may never know what he did wrong. Once the decision is made to pull the trigger on a deer, we owe it to them to make their death as quick and clean as possible.

I'm fortunate to only have wounded one deer in my life that I did not recover. I'm not being boastful about it, because I have surely missed more than my fair share. The one deer that I did wound was when I was 15 years old. Back then my father was working all the time and didn't get a chance to take me hunting very often. That particular Saturday, I was invited to hunt with a friend of dad's. Mac (George MacPherson) picked me up early in the morning and said we were going hunting up in Norway. At the time I didn't know where Norway, Maine, was and didn't really care as long as I could deer hunt.

We ate breakfast on the way at a diner, and then drove back in on a logging road just as it was breaking daylight. There was about eight inches of crusty snow on the ground making for noisy walking. Mac said we should sit on the ridge below the road, so we walked the road for a while and then split up to find places to sit. Obviously I didn't know the area, but neither did Mac, because he didn't have any specific spot in mind. I just walked around until I found some deer tracks and sat down. Back then I could sit for a long time, as that's how my dad told me to hunt. It seemed like I was just getting settled in when Mac came to get me. He said it was time to meet the other guys back at the truck for coffee. As we walked back up the ridge to the logging road, I was thinking how dumb it was to be going back to the truck already. So when we got up to the road, I told Mac that I would go up the ridge above it and walk back to the truck from there. Mac said that would be OK, so off I went.

I circled up the ridge and started walking parallel to the road, stopping every few steps to listen. I hadn't gone far when I heard crust breaking in front of me. As the sound got closer I could see a nice buck sneaking along in the firs with his head down. He was about 75 yards away and all I could see was flashes of him as he passed through openings. I could tell that the buck was heading for a good opening, so I aimed my 30-30 in the opening and fired just as his shoulder came into it.

At the sound of the gun, the buck jumped and disappeared back into the firs. I walked over to where he had been and found blood sprayed all over the snow. I got excited, sure the buck would be laying dead just ahead. I went down the track seeing blood sprayed everywhere, I thinking I must have hit the buck in the heart. But once I followed the trail 100 yards, I knew something was wrong. The blood had slowed down a bit, though it was still steady.

I came to where the buck had lain down and there was a lot of blood in his bed. I followed him all morning thinking he should run out of blood at any time. He was laying down every few hundred yards, but could hear me coming along in the crust. I don't know how far that buck took me, but eventually in the afternoon he crossed the road right where we had parked the truck that morning. The truck was gone, and I began to get a little nervous that the guys had left me there.

Of course the reality was that Mac thought I was lost and he was going to have to tell my dad! Now I figured I'd better wait right there for some help. The guys eventually showed up and were rightfully mad at me for disappearing. Remember, I was supposed to meet them for coffee about six hours ago. I told them what happened and showed them the track crossing the road. I think the guys had a hard time believing a 15-year-old kid tracked that buck all day.

Just then some local hunters came along and offered to help. An old guy said he "knew" the buck was going down into the swamp. He then offered to go on the track and help me. We didn't go far when we came to where the buck had lain down again. By now it was getting toward dark and the old timer said we should go down toward the swamp and look around. I wanted to stay on the track but figured this guy knew more than me. Needless to say we didn't see the buck. I was sure he would die in the night and that I would find him the next day if I could only get back in there. The problem was that both my father and Mac had to work the next day and I had no way to get back. To this day, losing that buck still bothers me. But I learned some important lessons from that experience.

Shooting ability and shot placement are the biggest factors in whether you are going have a clean kill or a wounded deer. Far too many hunters take shots that they are either not capable of making or shouldn't take in the first place. Other hunters just do not really know where to aim if a deer is at an odd angle or partially hidden by brush. I was guiding a client once who shot at a buck behind the shoulder when the buck was almost straight head on. The bullet hit the buck in the hind quarter. Fortunately, the buck only took a few jumps and stopped broadside, and my client's second shot did the job. When I asked him why he had aimed there, his explanation was that he had hit deer in the chest with buckshot when they were head on and never found them. The difference was that he was using a 30-06 this time.

Know your weapon and what it is capable of. Know its limitations, whether you hunt with a rifle, shotgun, muzzle loader or bow. And know what you are capable of doing with your weapon.

You also need to know the anatomy of a deer. There are several places to make a good killing shot other than the shoulder area, and knowing them will help you make quick decisions on where to aim when a deer is at any angle. It will also help you when the deer's shoulder is hidden from view. We have always been told to shoot a deer right behind the shoulder, taught that this is the best killing area, as the heart, lungs and liver are there. If you hunt in the wide open spaces, behind the shoulder is a good aiming point. I personally don't like that shot when hunting in the woods for a couple of reasons. One is that there is not a lot of room for error between a killing shot and being paunched or gut shot. This is especially true if the deer is quartering towards you slightly and you don't realize it. Deer that are paunched do not bleed very much and can travel a long way, making finding them a difficult task.

My buddy Marc Poirier learned that lesson on a nice buck in Ontario one year. He took a stand in the back of a clear-cut one morning during muzzle-loader season and hadn't been there very long when an eight-pointer wandered out of the woods about 100 yards away. When the buck stopped Marc settled the crosshair behind the buck's shoulder and squeezed off the shot. The buck took a few jumps and walked off like nothing had happened. Marc is an excellent shot and couldn't believe he had missed.

Chris and I heard the shot and went to give Marc a hand. Where the buck had been standing there were a few long gray hairs and a couple drops of blood. I knew the buck must be hit in the body because of the long hairs. I also knew that quite often there is no exit wound with a muzzle loader, so even if it was a good hit there might not be much blood initially. The puzzling part was that the buck walked off, which didn't correspond with a good hit.

There was a dusting of wet snow and we followed the buck about 100 yards without finding another drop of blood. When we got to the edge of the cut, the buck jumped up from just inside the wood line and ran off. Now I knew the buck wasn't hit where Marc thought and my guess was that he was paunched. The buck went into the thick cedars where there was no snow on the ground. Luckily the leaves were wet enough to see his tracks punched in them.

This is where a judgment call comes into play on whether to stay after the buck or let him have time to lie down and possibly die on his

Marc Poirier with his 215-lb. eight-point Ontario buck

own. I chose to stay after him. He didn't go far before he lay down the first time, and the odds of him going far again were slim. I also knew that what patches of snow there were in the openings would soon melt off. In the next few hundred yards we saw the buck several times. Finally I spotted him standing back to us in an opening 30 yards away. I told Marc to shoot the buck at the base of the tail, knowing it would break his back. At the shot, the buck dropped in his tracks. We discovered that Marc's first shot had hit him about 12 inches behind the shoulder and didn't hit the vitals. I'm sure glad that we were able to find that buck. I hate to think of how many deer are hit that way every year and never found.

I personally prefer to aim for the middle of the shoulder for several reasons. The number one reason is that there is a lot of room for error. In the woods there a lot of twigs and branches that you may not even notice when shooting. Hitting one can deflect a bullet off course. Aiming at the middle of the shoulder will also compensate for angles that you might not notice. In either case, you will have a much better chance of hitting the vitals. If you aim at the middle of the shoulder and hit high, you will hit the spine. If you hit low you will hit the heart. If you hit left or right you will get either the neck or the lungs and liver. All or these are good killing shots. The most important reason I like the shoulder shot is that breaking the shoulder bone limits a deer's ability to run and also sends bone fragments into the vitals, helping to ensure a quick death.

There are several other points on a deer that are good killing shots. When a deer is quartering towards you or away from you, visualize the bullet path crossing through the center of the deer's chest between the shoulders. This will make a good clean kill no matter what angle the deer is at. If a deer is head on, a shot dead center anywhere from the white patch on the deer's throat to the middle of the chest will get the job done. If a deer is back to, the best shot is the back of the neck or the base of the tail. If a deer is broadside and you don't have a shot at the shoulder, anywhere along the spine from the head to the tail will drop the deer in its tracks.

Some people might say that some of these shots are not ethical. I believe it's up to each individual hunter to make as clean a kill as possible. It is also up to each hunter to decide which shots they are willing or capable of taking. Knowing how to shoot a deer is the best way to prevent having to find a wounded one.

Eventually, even the best of intensions may end up going awry and you may find yourself looking for a wounded deer. Anytime I shoot at a buck and he doesn't go down within sight of me, I always go through the same steps to make looking for him easier. First, I think about how the buck reacted to the shot. Usually a deer hit in the heart and lung area will jump in the air and take off running full bore. That's a good sign; the deer will rarely make it 100 yards and most likely will be dead within 50. A deer shot in the paunch will usually hunch up and bound off. A deer shot in a leg with a broken bone will most likely stumble and possibly fall down. Then they scramble around trying to get moving on their three good legs. If the deer is running when you shoot, you may not see any reaction.

The reaction I pay the most attention to is when a deer drops in its tracks. When this happens, always keep your eye on the deer as you walk over to it. I've heard 100 stories about a deer getting up and running away when the hunter wasn't paying attention. These stories usually start with, "I thought he was dead" and end with the deer "got away."

I learned this lesson when I was a teenager, too. I was still hunting one day when the snow had turned to a cold rain. It was miserable weather, but as long as I was hunting I didn't care. I came down off from a hardwood ridge and started into some green growth when a doe jumped up from under a fir tree and ran for cover. I swung the gun on the doe and touched off a shot. She dropped like a sack of potatoes and was scrambling around on the ground.

I had never hit a running deer before, and I was pretty excited. Then, for some reason, I reached down to pick up my empty shell casing. When I straightened back up, I saw the doe running off into the brush. I couldn't believe it. I walked over to where the doe had been and couldn't find a drop of blood. I followed her for half a mile without ever finding any blood or the sign of a hit. The only thing I could think of was that the doe slipped in the wet snow when the gun went off. From that time on I have never taken my eyes off a deer until I was sure it was dead.

After I shoot at a buck, I always pick out the nearest tree or rock to the spot where the buck was and walk straight to it. I want to find where the buck was standing so I can look for hair and blood. Hair can give you an idea of what part of the body you may have hit. Short hair is probably from the lower part of the legs; white hair is probably from the belly. In either case, you know that the shot was low. Hair anywhere along the body will be similar except for on the brisket, where the hair is more coarse and bristly.

The only way body hair might help identify where you hit is if there is snow and you can see exactly where the deer was standing. The hair should drop to the ground in line with the hit. Usually there will only be a small tuft of hair. I you find a big wad of hair or a lot of hair scattered around, most likely you have just grazed the deer. It's kind of like running a hair clipper across your head and having it fall to the ground. Lots of hair is usually a sign that you did not hit the deer in a vital spot. I've only given one buck a haircut, and that monster is on my list of bucks that will always haunt me.

Quite often there will not be any blood where the deer was standing. If there is hair but no blood, it probably means the bullet didn't pass through. When a bullet passes through the body it will blow some blood out the far side. If there is snow on the ground it will be easy to follow the deer whether there is blood or not. On bare ground it is critical to go slow until you find blood. You may have to follow the deer by looking for tracks punched in the ground. Running tracks should be easy to follow, but focus on looking for blood.

If the blood is spraying off to the sides, the deer is hit in the lungs and will not be far away. This blood is going to be bright red and frothy looking. If the deer has traveled more than 100 yards and the blood is dripping straight down, it is most likely hit in a muscle and not the vitals. This blood is going to be dark red. Blood from a deer hit in the stomach or intestines will be watery.

If you follow a deer 100 yards without finding it dead, it's time to assess your next move. I'm going to assume the deer is not hit in the vitals and may only be wounded. By now there should be some indication of where the deer is hit. On bare ground the best option is to wait a while in hopes the deer will lie down. Once the deer lies down, it may not get back up. You also will have a better chance of getting another shot into the deer if it does get up again. If you come to a bed and the deer is gone, look for blood in the bed. The blood in the bed should tell you exactly where the deer was hit.

One night, my friend Stan Moody showed up at dinner and said he had hit a buck early that morning. Stan said the buck was running away when he shot, and he felt the buck was hit good. He had been tracking the buck most of the day and heard him walking in the crusty snow but could not get a look at him. Stan also said the buck had been bleeding the whole time. I told Stan I would go with him in the morning to see if we could get the buck. I suspected the hit was a flesh wound, but there was the possibility of a gut shot, and we owed it to the buck to find out.

The next morning Stan took me to where he had left the track. I followed the buck for a few hundred yards and came to his bed. The bed was frozen, so I knew we hadn't spooked the buck. There was a small spot of blood in the bed near the tail of the buck, which let me know that Stan had just made a flesh wound and the buck would survive.

If the blood is steady enough to follow along on it, hunt as though you were tracking the deer. Make sure to keep scanning the woods out in front of you, as a wounded deer might just stand and watch you long enough to offer another shot. If there is very little blood, you should mark each spot and search for the next. This can be slow and tedious, and you may eventually run out of blood. If that happens and you can't follow tracks, the only thing left to do is make searches. Try to think of the most logical place the deer would go and sweep back and forth as though you were still hunting.

This might also be the time to rally all your hunting partners to help with the search. To be effective with this type of search, everyone should form a line close enough together to be able to see in between one another. Then everyone should walk a straight line for a chosen distance, searching the ground between them for any sign of the deer. Once you go the chosen distance, everyone shifts over and you repeat the search in the opposite direction. The only person who does not change his/her position is the end person. This way, the end person (who knows where he/she has already searched) will know will keep the end line straight. These searches can be slow and tedious but it is probably your last chance of finding the deer.

The distance a buck travels after being hit, before lying down, is an indication of how bad he is hit. When a deer lies down soon after it is hit, most likely it is hit good enough to make the deer feel sick. If you hunt this deer slowly and give it time to lie down again, there is a good chance you'll get another shot or find him dead. But if a deer travels a long distance without lying down, the chances are that it is only a flesh wound. The only thing to do in this case is to follow the deer slowly in hopes getting another shot at him.

If there is snow on the ground, there is really no reason to wait before going after a wounded deer. If the deer has not lain down, the best bet is to hunt that deer as though it was not wounded. If you feel the deer is hit good or has a broken leg, the best bet is to pressure him hard and tire him out. The more tired he gets, the better your chance of getting another shot at him.

Mike Featherstone and I were tracking a buck together one muzzle-loader season in Maine. Mike was on the track and I was looping to one side. The buck crossed a stream and got with a doe in a thick stand of softwood. I knew that farther up the ridge it opened up into hardwoods. I worked my way up the ridge to the hardwood and started easing slowly along.

As I was coming over a rise I spotted Mike coming out of the firs off to my right. I knew the buck must have gone out into the hardwoods, so I kept easing up the rise one step at a time while scanning the woods ahead. Just then I spotted the buck across a ravine about 100 yards away. I was getting the bead on him when Mike fired. The shot surprised me, as I didn't know that Mike had seen the buck.

At the shot the buck started jumping around like he couldn't get anywhere. I thought Mike must have hit the buck good, but I decided to put a shot into him, just in case. The buck was jumping toward me, but just when I shot he jumped to one side and I knew that I had missed. Then the buck bounded off out of sight like nothing had happened. I thought to myself, that didn't look good. We reloaded our guns and walked over to figure out what had happened. We could see a little blood where the buck had jumped around in a circle. Then, where the buck bounded off, we could see that he was running on three legs.

Mike decided that he wanted to go right after the buck, so we took the track. The buck ran through the hardwoods for over half a mile until he got into some softwood again. Not far into the softwood, the buck jumped out his bed in front of Mike. There was no time for a shot.

The buck ran another half a mile and went into a real thick area of softwood. Mike kept seeing glimpses of him while I was trying to circle around in the thick firs. I bumped into Mike coming out the far side of the thicket on the track. The buck was heading up another hardwood ridge. I circled to the right, but the buck only went a couple hundred yards into the hardwoods, swung to the left and went back into the softwood thicket. We figured he must be getting tired and didn't want to be out in the open.

I had just split up with Mike to make a circle when I heard him shoot, so I went back over there. Mike said he had seen the buck's face looking at him through the firs, so he put the bead where he thought the buck's chest would be and fired. He missed the shot, so I started to circle again. It wasn't five minutes later that Mike shot again. When I walked back over to him, he told me that he had taken a running shot, as the buck jumped up in front of him. The buck had lain down only a short distance from where Mike had just shot at him, and we knew he was running out of steam.

I decided I might as well stay right with Mike since the buck wasn't going to be far away. We followed him down a ravine to a small stream. When Mike stepped up on a mound to see over the firs, the buck was laying in the stream 20 feet away. He stood up, exhausted, and Mike finished the job. His first shot had broken a front leg, just below the knee, and the buck didn't have the stamina to keep running on three legs.

Guide Mike Featherstone with the buck he calls "Mr. Smith."

In summary, by paying attention to these details, the job of finding a wounded deer will be a much easier task:

1. Watch the deer's reaction to the shot.
2. Mark the spot where the deer was standing.
3. Look for blood and hair.
4. Determine where the bullet hit.
5. Decide the best way to proceed on the trail.
6. Stay alert at all times.
7. Give it your best effort.

Hopefully, you will never have to use this chapter. But if you do, the information will give you your best chance of finding that wounded deer.

10

Tails From the Trail

THE ISLAND BUCK

When we started out on our first deer-hunting trip to Ontario, Canada, it was like an expedition into uncharted territory. Eight of us jammed into two Suburbans and headed west from Jackman, Maine in early December, not really knowing how long it would take to get to camp. Another one of the guys was going to fly in and meet us at camp. The group consisted of, myself and four of my guides at Cedar Ridge: Mike Featherstone, Mike Stevens, Kevin Harrison and Stan Moody. There were also three good friends: Chris Dalti (now my BWB partner/cameraman), Marc Pourier and Bob Sirpenski. Last but not least was my wife, Deb, to throw some grace into this motley crew.

To say that first drive out was the trip from Hell would be putting it mildly. We had estimated that it would take about 20 hours, so we decided to make the trip go nonstop. Thirty hours later, after enduring

The author poses with his first Ontario Big Woods Buck.

icy roads, snowstorms and running out of gas in the middle of the night, we finally rolled into camp. Camp was a cozy log cabin on the lake that we rented from a local guy named Steve, who we had met the previous summer while scouting the area.

After some much needed sleep, we awoke the next morning to find six inches of new snow on the ground. We were as excited as a bunch of kids in a candy store. Our plan was to hunt an island where Steve told us there were plenty of deer. The island was seven or eight square miles, so we were going to have plenty of room to spread out and look for tracks.

I had my mind made up that I was going to be particular about the buck I shot. After all, we had seen pictures of the big bucks that roamed this part of the country. We had brought along my snowmobile and a tote sled, thinking it might be handy to get a buck out of an area with roads that we couldn't drive a truck on.

As luck would have it, the lake was frozen over and we were able to get to the island with the snowmobile. I shuttled everyone to different spots around the island on the snowmobile, and with that done, I picked a spot for myself and headed into the canopy of thick spruce and fir.

It didn't take long to find deer tracks, but I couldn't find the monster buck track I was looking for. I walked a straight line for quite a while before finding a track that was bigger than what I had been

No one who was there will ever forget the first annual Cedar Ridge Guides Hunt in Ontario.

seeing. It still wasn't the type of track that gets my blood going, but I decided to follow it.

The track was hours old so I moved fast on it, the way I would on a track back home. To my surprise, I caught up to the buck in about 10 minutes; I heard him snort and run off. The buck had given me no indication that he might be lying down. I tracked him across the island, through thicket after thicket, all day long, hoping to get a decent look at him or find a bigger track to follow. Not having any luck with that, I made my way back to the lake at dark. After comparing notes with the guys in camp that night, we were all perplexed that with as many deer as there were, there didn't seem to be any big bucks. With no bucks on the pole that first day, we were going to have to get serious for tomorrow.

The next day, Kevin and Mike Featherstone both shot nice bucks. When we all arrived back at camp that night, those two bucks were the center of attention. They were the first Ontario bucks any of us had seen, and we checked them out from head to toe. We didn't have a scale, but we all agreed they would weigh 200 pounds or better.

The one thing about those bucks that caught our attention was the size of their feet. They were much smaller than those of the bucks back home with similar body size. Now we understood why we were not seeing the big bucks' tracks that we thought we should. In Maine, I could tell by a buck's track if he was the one I wanted to shoot. I knew the challenge now would be to get a good look at a buck to see if it was the one I wanted.

That week I saw quite a few bucks, but none of them had the antlers that I hoped to see. There were three other bucks taken and several more missed before five of the guys had to leave for home. I talked Mike Featherstone and Kevin into staying two more days so I could still search for a wall hanger. It didn't happen the next day, so I was down to one day left to hunt. I always say that the best hunt is when you can take it down to the last day and then score on a buck. I've got to admit, though, that I was putting a little bit of pressure on myself after letting all those bucks walk that week–especially since I had missed a monster buck with my muzzle loader back home the last day of the season.

The last morning of my hunt was not as cold as it had been, but the snow was now knee deep. I fired up the snow machine at daylight and headed out across the lake to the island that I was now becoming familiar with. Mike and Kevin would be relaxing again in the comfort of the cabin. On the trip out to the island, I was thinking that maybe there is something to be said for shooting a buck early in the hunt. I had figured out that the island was a deer yard. The bucks were not moving much now and most of them were holed up in the cedar thickets. My plan was the same as usual: find a good buck track and try to get a look at him. Today, though, I decided that if I could see a decent rack, I was going to shoot.

I left the snow machine on the edge of the lake and headed for a cedar swamp I knew of in the middle of the island. When I got within 100 yards of the swamp, I cut the track of a decent buck. He wandered into the swamp and began to feed on the cedar. Within 100 yards I came to his bed. The bed was frozen solid and he was up and feeding again. I knew this buck was not going to be too far away. I was excited about that, but not the fact that it was deathly still and seeing 20 yards in that swamp was a stretch. It was just one of those places where the only option is to jump the buck out and hope to catch him in a more open spot.

I eased along on the track expecting to hear the buck go crashing out at any time. Over the next hundred yards, the buck lay down five more times. Between each bed he was feeding on the cedar. The last bed was at the edge of the swamp, where it broke out into a more open area. This bed was not frozen and the buck's track was heading toward a low rocky ridge, which are common in that area. I felt confident that I was going to get a look at this buck and probably catch him feeding.

It was one of those days that you could hear a pin drop at 100 yards, so I was really going to have to put on the death creep. I crept up the ridge one step at a time, making sure to slowly compress the snow and not make a sound. Every step, I would stop to search behind every tree limb, rock and blow down. It probably took me an hour to go 30 yards. By that time, I could begin to see over the crest of the ridge. The buck had been feeding along its side, and I figured he would come back up on top of the ridge if he was going to lie down, so I stayed on top where I would have a better view.

I had eased along about 10 more steps when I spotted the top of the buck's rack behind a log, about 15 yards away. All I could see of the rack was the top of the points and the tip of the beam, but it was enough to know that it must be a 10-pointer. The buck was lying down watching his backtrack where it crossed over the top of the ridge. I didn't dare to take another step, so I stretched up and then I could see about four inches of the top of the buck's back. I knew the snow was at least a foot deep on the log, and I thought about shooting through the snow where his shoulder would be. Then I figured, with my luck, I would hit a branch hidden in the snow. So I eased my rifle up and stretched again until I could make out his back. I put the bead on his spine and touched off the shot. The buck never got out of his bed. That hunt could not have played out any better. Although he was not the monster buck I was hoping for, he's still a trophy to me. My first Ontario buck hangs proudly on my wall.

The author shot this buck while still-hunting on his scrape line.

THE SCRAPE-LINE BUCK

It was our second early-season hunt in Ontario. Unlike the year before when the weather was cool with some dustings of snow, this year was a little warmer–not too warm, but more seasonal than the previous year. It was the pre-rut period and the bucks were really laying down the sign. The buck sighting had been good so far that week. After hunting this area for three years (2 early and 1 late season), the guys in the group were really getting particular about the bucks they wanted to shoot. After three days of hunting, there had been plenty of deer stories, but there was only one buck on the pole. What a buck it was, though, a typical 12-point with two sticker points. The honors for that buck went to Lee Libby. It was Lee's first trip to Ontario, but it definitely was not going to be his last. Lee's buck had really lain down the gauntlet for the rest of us, and we knew we better get serious.

Once again this year, Chris was following me with a video camera, hoping to get some good footage. We had been hunting the same area for a few days, and I couldn't get my mind off the big non-typical buck that I had missed the first morning. Neither Chris nor I had been able to count the number of points on that buck's rack, but we both concurred that there were plenty. That first morning of the hunt, I was so sick with some kind of virus that I couldn't get out of bed. By nine o'clock I was feeling better, so we jumped in the truck and made our way up to a new area we wanted to hunt.

The area had been being logged the year before, so I knew it had good potential for deer this year. We stopped to scout a place where the new clear-cuts bordered an older clear-cut, grown up with head-high jack pines. Many of the clear-cuts in that area have low rolling ridges and are great places to still hunt. The pines are good cover and the tops of the ridges offer good vantage points to spot from. Some of the cuts are huge and you can see as far as you can shoot.

As we crested the first ridge, I could see a buck standing in the jack pines on the next ridge over. His whole body stood out like a beacon from the sun shining on his tan hair. I motioned to Chris as I brought my binoculars up. As soon as I focused the binoculars on the buck's antlers, I knew there was no question about shooting him. I brought the Omega to my shoulder and put the bead on the buck. The bead covered most of his body, and it didn't dawn me that he was farther away than I thought.

I centered the bead on the buck's shoulder and touched off the shot. The buck just bounded into the pines and disappeared. I knew right then that I had missed. To make it a double goof, Chris told me that I hadn't waited for his cue that the camera was rolling. After I reloaded my gun, we headed over to check for any sign of a hit. I paced off the distance to where the buck had been standing at 200 yards. I'm usually a pretty good judge of distance, but I really messed up this time. I'd thought the buck was about 100 yards away, but I should have realized that the bead wouldn't cover that much of a deer's body at that distance. I was sure that I shot right under the buck. That buck was the biggest-rack buck I had ever had a chance to shoot, and he's on the top of my list of bucks that haunt me by getting away.

After a few fruitless days of trying to find the same buck, we decided to try the island for a change of scenery. Kevin Harrison and Chris Krukowski (another guide and good friend) had hunted the island the day before and said the sign looked good. We loaded into the boat at daylight for the journey across the lake. Kevin and Chris were going back to the same area they had been hunting at one end of the island. I told them to drop us off in the middle of the island and we would hunt a circle towards them.

It was cool at daylight, but as the sun rose it started to warm up. We still hunted all morning looking for the rubs and scrapes that would tell us where the bucks were hanging out. At 10 o'clock we were in an area that had plenty of good buck sign, so it was time to have a sandwich. Chris and I sat down against the same tree, each looking a different direction. By now it was about 50 degrees and the sandwich made me a little sleepy.

I was leaning back against the tree with my eyes closed when I could hear hooves pounding the ground coming from Chris's direction. I didn't dare to move; I just opened my eyes and waited. A doe came running by us at about 10 feet and stopped 20 yards away to look back. I heard hooves coming again and this time I had my gun ready, thinking it could be a buck following the doe. No such luck. It was another doe heading straight for us. That doe came so close, Chris was afraid it was going to jump on his legs, so he waved his arms and the doe ran around behind us. We stayed right there and waited for another half hour, thinking there might be a buck chasing the does, but none showed up.

We continued still hunting along, finding plenty of good buck rubs. There was enough sign to know that the law of averages would have to catch up to us and we'd see a buck. It wasn't long before I realized we were near where I had shot the island buck the first year we hunted there. I got out my GPS to see how close we were to the spot, and it said about 300 feet. I could see a ridge in front of us, and I knew it had to be the right place.

We worked our way up onto the open ledges, and as soon as we got to the top, Chris called for a water break. Fifty feet from us there was a higher ledge, so I said let's go over there and take a break. We had no more than got to the other ledge when we both heard some scuffling to our left. A buck had walked out onto the ledge and stopped 30 yards from us and behind some fir trees. I could see the body of the buck, but not his rack. Chris said he saw the rack and it looked pretty good. I waited for the buck to take a step ahead, but the he must have sensed us and ran back the way he came.

When the buck jumped through an opening, I could see that he was big and had a tall-tined rack. I swung my gun on the buck and fired just as he disappeared into the firs. After a careful search, I concluded that it was a clean miss. When I fired at the buck, he was jumping down off the ledge, so I must have shot over him. Well, now I was 0 for 2 on bucks for the week.

We continued still hunting in the direction the buck had run and eventually came to another series of ridges. These ridges were fairly open and I had hunted them before. They were steep on the sides but flat and easy walking on top–the kind of ridges that made it perfect for still hunting, as the mossy ledges were quiet walking and the steep sides were good to peer over in hopes of catching a buck lying down. We had been working these ridges for a while, looking in every nook and cranny, and were just cresting a ridge when a buck jumped up in front of us and bounded down a ravine. He was only 40 yards away and in the open, and we could see that he was just an average-sized eight-pointer. Not being the kind of buck I was looking for, we just watched him bound gracefully away. There is something about a close encounter with any buck in the big woods that puts me in awe of this amazing creature.

We sat down and had our afternoon sandwich break while reflecting on the day's events. In this type of country, seeing one nice buck in a day is something, but seeing two was a bonus. We only had a couple of hours left until dark, so we hunted our way towards the lake. To get to there, we had to drop down off the ledges and into the low ground where the woods were a lot thicker. As we worked our way down a ravine, we came upon several scrapes in one spot. The scrapes were made along a deer trail that was paralleling the ravine. I knew the best chance for seeing a buck would be to follow the deer trail.

As we followed the trail along, we kept finding more scrapes and rubs. This was getting pretty exciting; I slowed down the pace to a crawl. When the trail turned across a narrow swale bog, I could see the lake out in the distance. At the other side of the swale where the trail entered the woods, there was a fresh scrape and a rub on a three-inch fir tree. We took a few minutes to capture that sign on tape and then continued on the trail.

I was easing along one step at a time while the trail went up a low knoll. Just as I crested the knoll, I spotted a buck coming head on down the trail right towards us. He was only 30 yards away across an opening, but did not see us. I knew in this situation I was going to have to make a quick decision about shooting. The buck put his head down and I eased the Omega into my shoulder. I could see that his antlers had a good spread, but were not overly tall. The buck would not turn his head, so I couldn't see how many points he had.

Then I heard Chris say "take him," which means the camera is rolling and I can shoot. I knew this buck wasn't going to stand around all day, so when he picked up his head I touched off the shot. At the sound of the shot, the buck dropped in his tracks. When I turned to Chris for a high five, I noticed the camera was still in his coat. Chris said he was so excited and didn't want the buck to get away, he said "take him" without thinking about the camera. It's funny what a big buck will do to a hunter's mind, even one with a camera.

When we walked over to where the buck lay, I was pretty excited. He was a nice sleek buck with a symmetrical eleven-point rack. He had good beams and a good spread, a real trophy in my book. I always talk about two points connecting and this time the points were dead on. The buck had been walking down the scrape line we had been hunting on, and I'm sure he made some of the scrapes we had been seeing along the way. By the time we did some filming and took photos, it was getting late. The good news was that it was only 100 yards to the lake and it was going to be an easy drag. We got to the lake just in time to watch the sun set over the water as we waited for our boat ride back to camp. When Kevin showed up in the boat to pick us up, he told us that he had shot a nice 10-point early that morning. With two bucks on the pole, there was some storytelling and celebrating that night.

THE SWALE-BOG BUCK

This was to be our first early-season "Guides Hunt" to Ontario. The previous year's late-season hunt was cold and the snow was deep. Most of the big bucks had shed their antlers, making it discouraging to say the least. Not wanting to risk that happening again, we all decided to try something different. I had heard from Steve, our regular Ontario host, that there had been an early snow a few days before we were to arrive. October snows do not usually last very long, but I was hoping there might still be some on the ground when we arrived.

As we were driving closer to camp, we began to see snow on the ground. We were all pretty excited about being able to do some tracking that early in the season. That night in camp we made the plan that half the guys would go north and half would go south and try to find some buck tracks.

The author shot this buck as it was feeding on moss after an all-day tracking job.

I was in the south contingency with Chris Dalti, Marc Poirier and Lee Shanze. We decided to try an area where I had found some deer the year before. As we drove down the main logging road, we could see plenty of tracks crossing it. Most of the tracks were in some stage of being melted out. There was only an inch or two of wet snow, and it looked as though it would probably melt off that day.

We finally turned onto a mud road that led to the back of a clear-cut. About halfway through the cut, there was a track crossing the road. We all jumped out of the truck to check it out. The track looked like that of a decent buck and the best part was that it was real fresh. We stood there looking at the track and then at each other, knowing we were all thinking the same thing. Who's going to take this track? The conversation usually goes something like this: "You want to take it?" "I'll take it, but do you want it?" "I'll take it if you don't want it. It's up to you." "No, it's up to you."

I think most of you trackers can relate to this. Sometimes it can end up with a coin toss. This time Lee ended it with, "You take it." It was going to be the first attempt at videoing for Chris and me, so Lee figured it would be our best chance of getting some footage. It sure is great having good hunting buddies.

Marc and Lee said good luck and drove off to look for another track heading towards the wood line 100 yards away. The buck was wandering and feeding in the cut, so I knew it wouldn't take long to catch up to him. This time of the year the bucks are usually not traveling very far. When we got into the woods, the ground was mostly bare from the snow melting out of the trees. I decided instead of trying to follow the track on bare ground, I would circle the bare spots and pick up his track coming out. That would let me spend more time trying to spot the buck.

We were circling the first bare spot back towards the cut when the buck jumped out of the thick brush 30 yards from us. As he ran out into the cut, I could see antlers through the brush, but they didn't appear to be very big. I snorted at the

A buck that loses his antlers during the season is safe for another year. (Sue Morse photo)

buck as he ran up onto a knoll and he stopped on top of it. His body looked good sized, but his head was behind a fir tree and I couldn't see his rack. I grunted at him to see if he would step into the open where I could get a better look at him. The buck wasn't interested in what I had to say and bounded away.

It was shaping up to be a good day. We were only a half hour into the day and already had a buck jumped. With quiet walking and wet snow, I was confident we would get a chance to see that buck again. Since tracking was going to be slow because of the bare ground, I decided to only wait a few minutes before taking up the track. I told Chris that I wasn't going to shoot at the buck unless I got a better look at his rack. Chris said he'd keep the camera ready and we headed out on the track.

The buck went back into the woods and then worked his way toward a swale bog. He walked the edge of the bog for a ways and then went back into the woods. Because the buck began to wander again, I was easing along very slowly. When the buck went out into the swale again, I thought for sure that I would catch him in it. No such luck. He turned back into the woods again.

Just as we started into a fir thicket, the buck jumped and ran out of it, giving me glimpses of brown to see. After spooking the buck once more, I decided to have a sandwich, wait half an hour and take up the chase again.

The buck led us out into a clear-cut that was grown up with head-high poplar trees. He worked his way down the edge of the cut to a strip of woods. I could see another swale bog though the woods and the buck's track was going towards it. We were easing through the strip of woods when a deer snorted on the other side of the bog. I snorted back at it, and we stood and waited. A few minutes later a doe stepped out into the bog and walked towards us. Just then, another deer snorted back in the woods from where the doe had come from. I expected the buck to step out any minute. But minutes later, the doe bounded back into the woods.

The woods became quiet while we waited to see if the buck would show. After a few minutes, we worked our way out into the bog. At the edge of it there was another buck track crossing the one we were on. Both bucks had gone out into the bog, where the ground was bare. I was scouring the ground, trying to figure out where our buck had gone, when Chris said, "There he goes."

There was a high beaver dam to our right and the swale below the dam was only about 50 yards wide. The buck bolted across the swale from behind the dam and all I saw was one jump before he disappeared into the woods again. Chris said he had seen the buck's rack and it looked good to him. That's just what I wanted to hear. I went over to check where the buck had been and saw that he had been feeding on some old man's beard. I decided not to wait around in hopes of catching him feeding again.

The buck only ran about 100 yards and started walking again. He definitely had a death wish! He went out across the same clear-cut he had just been in and into the woods on the other side. Now there would be no more sizing up his rack; it was time to shoot if the chance came.

Not long after we entered the woods from the cut, the chance came for a shot. When the buck jumped up in front of us again, I swung the Omega on him and fired as he jumped between two spruce trees. When the smoke cleared everything was quiet. I thought for sure that I had hit the buck. I reloaded the smokepole and we went over to check it out. But after following the track for 50 yards, it was apparent that I had missed.

I had yet to shoot a running buck with a muzzle loader, and I guessed this hunt was going to be trial and error. We continued on the

The hunters had every right to be proud of these three nice 200+ lb. Ontario muzzle-loader bucks.

buck as he went over a ridge and down to another swale bog. This bog was grown in with alders and patches of firs. We were easing one step at a time towards the bog when the buck busted out from behind a wall of firs 30 feet in front of us. I got lined up on him and fired again, just as he disappeared into the alders. This time I didn't feel as good about the shot, as there were a lot of alders to shoot through. We went over to check, but couldn't find any sign of a hit. I figured that buck must be spooked after being shot at twice, so I decided another sandwich break was in order.

As we ate our sandwiches, I told Chris that I had never seen a buck act like this one. The buck did not seem to be too worried that something was following him, and I was sure we would get another chance at him. With lunch done, we got back on the track. Again the buck only ran a ways and started feeding on the edge of the bog. The swale had a sharp bend in it and we eased around it, expecting to see the buck at any time. Around the corner the swale narrowed to about 30 yards and I could see the buck's track leading across it and into the woods on the other side.

I could hear sticks breaking in the woods where the track disappeared. Then I saw movement behind a blow down back in the woods. It was quite thick in there, and I kept watching until I finally saw antlers moving around. The buck was feeding on the old man's beard hanging from the blow down. I could have poked a bullet through, but I knew I had to wait for a better chance to get video footage.

Finally the buck worked his way closer to the bog again and started to feed on another blow down 30 yards away, but he still was not in the clear for the camera. I'd now watched this buck for 15 minutes without shooting, and the filming was starting to get to me; I'm not used to waiting around for a shot. Then the buck took one step ahead and put his body in the open. When I touched off the shot, the cloud of smoke hung in front of me in the damp air. Then I heard Chris saying, "You got him! You got him!" At last we were going to get that close-up view of the buck that we had been waiting for.

We found him lying dead 20 yards from where he'd stood–another nice Ontario 10-pointer with a perfectly symmetrical rack. Chris I both agreed that the buck would field dress over 200 pounds.

By now it was getting late in the day and we had just enough time to take photos and roll some video tape before the drag out. I knew the boys would be happy to have meat on the pole the first day in camp.

RACKASAURUS

Our first muzzle-loader hunt in Ontario was winding down. The week had been a good one so far. There were three bucks on the pole, each over 200 pounds. All of the guys in camp had had a chance at a buck but were holding out for bigger ones. I had taken the swale-bog buck the first day and was still looking to find a bigger one. In Ontario there is a "party hunting" system that allows anyone in a group of hunters to tag a buck shot by another member of the group. Chris wanted me to use his tag on the swale-bog buck so we could try and get more video footage of me hunting. I knew that was a big sacrifice for him and I didn't take it lightly.

The snow we hunted in on the first day was all but gone by the second day, ending our chances for any serious tracking. The weather had stayed fairly cool that week and the buck activity was really picking up. Every day more scrapes and rubs were showing up in the woods, and almost every day Chris and I hunted a different area, trying to learn as much of the country as we could.

At 280 lbs. dressed weight, with a B&C score of 166 1/8, "Rackasaurus" is the author's biggest buck to date.

The next-to-the-last day of the hunt, we went to another new area that looked good on the map. Chris was coming down with a head cold, so I told him we would take it easy that day; we had put on a lot of miles that week scouting. The area we were going to try was about a mile wide on a peninsula in the lake. It was all big timber with no clear-cuts. As soon as we started into the woods that morning, we began seeing fresh rubs. Either there were going to be a lot of bucks there or we just got lucky and stumbled into a hot spot.

We still hunted along, following the buck sign, until we came to a fairly high ridge. The ridge had moss-covered ledges and looked like a perfect place to sneak up on a buck. But we hunted that ridge and several more like it without seeing a single deer.

I decided to move down into some lower ground and find a swale to hunt around. In these big-timber areas there is not very much feed and the deer are drawn to the swale bogs, where the feed is better. We hunted down a ravine for a while until I starting seeing some buck sign again. I followed a deer trail around a knoll and right to a fresh scrape–a big annual scrape pawed into the black dirt. The track in the scrape was huge, and the scrape was in the intersection of several trails. As I began looking around, I could see rubs everywhere. It was evident that several bucks were traveling through this area. We had found one of those places a deer hunter dreams about.

All of a sudden we heard footsteps coming down the knoll. A doe came into view and stopped 30 yards from us. I could feel a breeze on the back of my neck, and I knew she was going to catch our scent. Sure enough, she snorted and ran down off the knoll and disappeared. I snorted at her as she ran and she stopped and snorted back. We snorted back and forth at each other for a few minutes and then all was quiet.

Chris and I waited around a while hoping that a buck might come along, but nothing showed. I was thinking about what to do next when I realized Chris was not looking too good. His ears were so plugged up that he was having a hard time walking quietly and we were not going to have much chance of sneaking up on a buck. I decided to get him back to camp so he could get some rest, knowing this was going to be the place to hunt tomorrow.

We awoke the next morning to a dusting of snow covering the ground. It looked like enough to be able to track. The last day of the hunt was looking like a good one. Chris's cold was not getting any better and he decided to stay back in camp, unwilling to cut down my chances at a buck. Most of the guys had their last day spots all picked out, but Tom said he would try my spot. So we dropped Lee off at his spot on the way down the road.

Tom and I planned on starting about a mile apart and circling towards each other. He dropped me off on a ridge that ran along a swale bog, and then he disappeared down the road. I was about half a mile from where we had seen all the buck sign the day before and was going to hunt my way in that direction.

I worked my way down the ridge in hopes of finding a good buck track to follow. I had hunted about half a mile and was surprised that I hadn't even seen a doe track. I could see another ridge on the other side of the swale, so I worked my way around the end of it to get to there. As I started up that ridge through the hazel nut brush, I heard a deer bust out in front of me. On my way over to where the sound came from, I cut a buck track and followed it to a good-sized bed.

I was feeling pretty lucky to stumble onto a bedded buck, and a good one at that. I had just sat down to wait my half hour when a shot rang out in the direction the buck had gone. I thought it must have been Tom, as he was in the direction the shot had come from. I called him on the radio and he said that it wasn't him shooting. We knew people were baiting deer along the road in that area and figured it must have been them who shot. I knew this buck wouldn't be going to feed on bait, but my curiosity was getting to me.

I got on the buck's track and he took me straight towards where the shot had come from. I was beginning to get a sinking feeling that someone had shot him, but I thought at least I would get to see what he looked like. Pretty soon I could hear voices coming from in front of me. The buck had followed a trail past a bait pile and there was a little blood in the snow. I caught up to the voices expecting to see a dead buck. There were two guys, and one said he had hit the buck good and they were tracking it. I told them good luck and headed away from the direction they were going. I knew I was only about 100 yards from the road again because that's where the baits were. My plan now was to get back in as far from the road as I could.

I went about a quarter of a mile and cut another buck track, heading in the direction I wanted to go. Things were looking up again. I wasn't sure if it might be the buck the other hunters were tracking, as it came from that direction, but there was no blood so I was going to follow it anyway. About 50 yards down the track, I came to a scrape. Now I was sure this wasn't the buck the other hunters were following. I followed this buck up onto a knoll and right to a huge scrape. When I was looking the scrape over, I found two sets of buck tracks leaving it. It was easy to see why there was a scrape there. It was an intersection of two deer trails crossing on top of the knoll. I wanted to make sure that both sets of tracks weren't made by the same buck circling. I followed both sets out for a ways–far enough to know they were made by two different bucks. I decided I better call Tom to tell him, so he could take one of the tracks.

I was standing beside the scrape when I called Tom. I had just started to explain what I found when I heard a snap and then the telltale sound of an antler hitting a branch. I looked up the knoll just in time to see the flash of a big rack in the firs at about 75 yards and coming towards me. That one flash was enough to know this was a real good buck. He stopped behind some firs at about 50 yards. I could see his outline, but I only had one shot and knew I had to make it count.

The buck started running again and was quartering towards me, but all I could see was glimpses of him through the firs. The closer the buck got, the more I knew things were going to happen fast. There was a thick spruce tree in front of me, blocking my view, so as the buck jumped behind another patch of firs, I took a step to the left and put the gun up. I was sure the buck was going to cross an opening to my left, so I gave a loud bleat. Just as the buck jumped into the opening, he stopped as if on cue. I put the bead on his shoulder and touched off the shot. The buck jumped into the air, bolted off and ran out of sight.

I couldn't believe what had just happened. It's a rare day when a big buck runs right towards you in the big woods. At that point I didn't know if the buck had five points or 25, but I knew his rack was big. I pulled out my radio again and called Tom to tell him what had happened, and his reply was, "You're welcome." At the time I hadn't known what he meant, but I knew that I was going to find out.

It was only 19 paces to where the buck had stood and there was a good blood trail heading in the direction he had gone. I followed the blood trail 30 yards to the edge of the knoll and could see my buck lying dead under some firs. I took one look at his antlers and couldn't believe what I was seeing. They were heavy and dark, with long beams, and the spread was out well past his ears. I called Tom again to say I'd found the buck and he said he was coming on the track. When he got to me and saw the buck, I think he was more in awe than I was. Then he told me why he'd said, "You're welcome." He had jumped the buck but had not been able to see his antlers very well, so he didn't shoot. Talk about two points connecting again. We were only 200 yards apart when he jumped the buck and the buck happened to run in my direction. So I'm indebted to Tom for that buck.

Tom said there was a little blood in the buck's track and he thought it might be the one that the other guy hit. When we dragged my buck down the knoll to a flat area to take pictures, we noticed that he had a broken front leg just below the knee. As we were taking pictures, we heard voices and the same two guys I had seen earlier turned up. They had followed Tom's track down to us. I showed the guy where he had hit the buck and I could see the disappointment in his face. The guys then left and Tom and I finished our photo session. I was glad to have been able to save that buck from the wolves, which was sure to be his fate. With the snow almost gone, there would be no way to catch up to a buck with a wound like that.

Tom was guessing the buck to weigh 285 pounds, but I was more conservative with my guess and said 250 pounds. One thing we were both sure of, though, was that we were going to need help getting him out. We had some uphill dragging ahead of us and I was trying to get through the season with a hernia. Tom went back to camp for help while I did the field dressing chore. As I waited for help to arrive, it was great to be able to sit in the woods and reflect on the events of the week and how it all ended. I also thought about how blessed I was to be able to be there with such a great group of friends.

Tom had called Lee on the radio to tell him about my buck, and Lee said he would come and help. He ended up walking a couple of miles down the road until he could reach me on the radio. We wondered what was taking so long for the guys to get back, until we learned that Mike Stevens had shot a buck and they had been helping him with it. Tom finally arrived back with the reinforcements and led them back in to where I was waiting. I think the guys were more excited than I was when they saw the buck. Lee said, "That's a rack-asaurus," and that's the name that stuck. After all the back slapping and hand shaking, it was time to get the old boy back to camp and on the pole.

This buck saved the life of the big one the author was tracking.

JR

It was the last day of muzzle-loader season in Maine, and there was finally some new snow on the ground. About three inches of powdery snow had fallen in the night and it was still spitting fine flakes. The temperature was around zero and the wind was blowing a pretty good clip. It was just the kind of weather that keeps a lot of hunters inside drinking coffee. I knew this was going to be the best chance of killing a buck that I'd had all week. I figured there was enough wind and new snow to make it quiet going. I always call them, "deer killing days"!

As usual, this was my one week to hunt for myself in Maine, as I guide clients the four weeks of rifle season. It had been tough tracking that week–cold and calm with a crusty snow. Chris was following me with the video camera in hopes of getting film of me taking a Maine buck. The day before we had tracked a buck that took us to an area that appeared to be "Buckville." There were good buck tracks crisscrossing a hardwood ridge in all directions. The ridge was surrounded by thick green growth and swamps–just the kind of place that bucks like to call home–and that was the spot where we would be going. I was sure we could pick up a good track in that area.

We ate breakfast, I got my good-luck kiss from Deb, we grabbed our lunches and headed out the door. I couldn't help but think that Deb had to be relieved it was the last morning she would have to get up at 3:30 to cook breakfast this year. It's a long fall, but she manages to keep the troops fat and happy!

We pounded the truck down the icy logging roads as close as we could to the ridge. Then we gathered our gear and began the long walk back in. I kept up a good pace, as all I was trying to do was find a good buck track to follow. We had walked a ways and were going through a cedar bog when we cut a small buck track. A little farther on we cut a pretty good track, partly filled in with snow. It was going towards the ridge, so I followed it.

The buck had worked his way out of the bog and started up the ridge. I could see another set of tracks up ahead of us. I hurried up there to find just what I was looking for: the track of a buck that looks like a cross-country skier. He had a 12-inch stance and was dragging his feet through the snow. The track had very little snow in it, so I knew it had been made late in the night.

I started along on the track and had only gone about 100 yards, when another buck track crossed it. This track was just as big and it was even fresher. I figured that it couldn't be more than a couple of hours old. Things were starting to get pretty exciting. We switched to that buck and followed him down the ridge. He crossed a stream and was heading off in a straight line. We went along at a steady walk, knowing the buck could be miles away. Then the buck crossed an old logging road and worked his way up another ridge.

We were working our way through a softwood thicket when we came to his bed. He had given me no indication that he was going to lie down and the direction of his bed told me that he wasn't watching his backtrack. Now I knew this buck was tired and wasn't paying attention behind him, and the odds of getting a look at him seemed pretty good. There was no snow in his bed, and my first thought was that we had jumped him. I felt the bed and it was frozen, so I knew the buck was up and traveling again. I told Chris to have the camera ready; there was going to be some action.

The buck stayed on a straight line until he got to an old chopping that was grown in with head-high whips. There he starting zigzagging like he was searching for a doe. We had not seen another deer track from the time we crossed the old logging road, and there had been snow on the ground for over a week. The buck must have known there was a doe around the chopping at one time and he was trying to find her. His track then went out into the chopping and headed straight across it.

The wind was whipping across the chopping and drifting snow into the track. I was trying to look as far down the track as I could see when Chris said he saw a deer on the far side of the chopping, behind a blow down. I could see a blown-down log in the hardwoods and was concentrating on looking there, but could not see a deer. Then Chris said it was a buck. I still couldn't see anything, and realized that I was looking too far away. On the far side of the chopping, about 100 yards away, there was a clump of winter beech. The brown leaves on them don't drop off for most of the winter. When the buck stepped out of the beech, I finally got my eye on him. He was about 100 yards away, with his head down, and walking right towards us through the whips. I couldn't believe this luck; the buck was coming back in his track. I couldn't see his rack very well, but knew it was the width of his ears. I didn't really care, as a track that big was going to be a big old buck.

Chris said he had the camera rolling and I could shoot when I wanted. I knew the buck wasn't going to see us, so I got the Omega to my shoulder and waited for him to pick his head up. From then on, I never looked at his rack again. When the buck was about 50 yards from us he stopped and picked his head up. I instantly put the bead on his chest and fired. At the shot the buck ran straight toward us. At about 20 yards away he slowed down and stopped. He was wobbling back and forth, trying to stay on his feet. That's when it struck me that this couldn't be the buck we had been tracking. This buck had a thin basket rack and his body did not match the size of the track. I was staring in disbelief as the buck took a few more steps and went down. I turned to Chris to tell him that it wasn't the buck we were on, but he had already figured it out himself.

As we walked over to the buck, I was running through my mind what could have happened. Did I misjudge the track? No, I looked at the buck's hoof and it was quite a bit smaller than the one we had been tracking. I wondered where this buck came from, as there were no other tracks around. I just figured it was a coincidence that the two bucks crossed paths and this buck was walking in the other buck's track. It made sense, though, because when there is a crust on the snow, it's easier for a deer to walk in another one's track instead of breaking through the crust. This buck was just in the wrong place at the wrong time.

I told Chris the good news was that we were only a couple of hundred yards from another old logging road that we could get the truck to. By the time we took our photos and some video footage we were starting to get pretty cold. I don't think it had warmed up a degree all day. I didn't waste any time field dressing the buck out so we could get moving again. We dragged him down to the logging road and left him there while we headed back to get the truck, which was about two miles away. When got to the truck and starting driving around to get the buck, I told Chris we would probably see the big buck track crossing the road.

Sure enough, when we were almost back to where we left the buck there were tracks coming off the ridge and crossing the road. I was surprised that there were three sets of tracks. The big buck was with a doe with a lamb (fawn). The wind was blowing down the road and the tracks were not drifted in, so they must have just crossed the road.

Now I was able to piece together the whole story. The buck I shot had been staying on that ridge with the doe and lamb. They must have been there since the snow because there were no other tracks coming or going into there and we had circled the whole area. The big buck found them and ran the smaller buck off. That's why he was coming down the big buck track; to leave the area. When I shot, the big buck had to be within a quarter of a mile from us. We had been at least two hours getting the truck and coming around, and the tracks in the road were not that old. Although I didn't shoot the buck I was after, it was a great hunt and I'm glad to have my little buck. I call him junior, or JR for short. It just goes to show you, that you can never tell what might happen when you're on the trail of a buck.

11

Down the Road

In the five years since my I wrote my last book, I have been amazed at the number of hunters with the interest in the big woods. I used to think that the big woods hunter was a small contingent of us dyed-in-the-wool New Englanders. Since that time, I have discovered that there are not only big woods hunters all across the northern tier, but the interest lies everywhere there are deer hunters. I think there is something magical about hunting in the snowy woods of the North Country. To many hunters, the opportunity to track a buck in the big woods is a life-long dream.

Over last few years, I have had the opportunity to talk to big woods trackers from Maine to Minnesota and we all seem to share the common bond going one-on-one with a big woods buck on his own turf. The terrain and woods change from one area to another, but the solitude of being on a track does not. To someone who hasn't been there, it's hard to explain what the solitude of the big woods is like.

With the success of my first book, the idea was born to start a business dedicated to teaching hunters, new and old alike, the ways of the big woods. I have done this by giving seminars at various sporting events as well as teaching classes at my outfitting business. Along with Chris, I have also produced a DVD and tracking cards--which are a big hit with hunters. I will continue with this endeavor as long as there are hunters willing to learn.

I hope somehow this book has either inspired you to hunt the big woods or, if you already have, it has helped you fill in that missing piece of the puzzle. So get in the woods and may our paths cross on some remote mountain ridge.

You can contact me through our website: bigwoodsbucks.com

AFTERWORD

Peter Fiduccia asked me to write a "special contribution" for Big Woods Bucks: Vol. 2. This is an honor. I certainly didn't anticipate that I would be penning this when I first met Hal Blood in 1989.

While attending the annual Eastern Fishing and Outdoor Expo in Worcester, Massachusetts, that year with my hunting buddy Marc Poirier, we met Hal at the show and, after talking for a while, we booked a hunt with him for that fall. As we would later discover, we were his first guided clients. When we arrived in the fall, Hal mentioned that he had killed a huge buck he nicknamed "Thin Horns." We were convinced the decision to hunt with Hal was right on the money.

I had no idea I was starting a friendship with the kind of a person I would come to respect and feel honored to know. Hal has helped me and countless other deer hunters sharpen our hunting and woodsman skills to become one with the wildlife in the woods. I have never met a man who is as persistent (I call it stubborn) as he is. He doesn't have a lazy bone in his body and works until he nearly drops in order to put a client on a buck.

Let me describe a few of those moments.

On a windswept rainy day, we were scouting/still-hunting a three-mile-long peninsula that jutted out into a huge lake in western Ontario. We stalked to within 10 yards of a mature doe lying down tucked behind a blow down and observed her body language, learning what she reacted to as her ears scanned the swale in front of her like radar dishes on a battleship.

On another hunt, about 2,000 feet above sea level on the side of a mountain in western Maine, miles from the nearest road, Hal and I searched for the square-toed track of one of those legendary monster bucks Maine is so well known for. We never cut the size track we were looking for that day, but we did come upon an amazing scene unfolding right before our eyes. Four bull moose had answered the moaning call of a cow moose in estrus. The bulls spent the next 45 minutes courting the cow, shoving and sparring with each other, breaking trees up to two inches in diameter like they were twigs.

Perched in a treestand Hal had strategically placed in the notch of two mountains in Maine, I passed up shooting a medium-sized black bear at six o'clock p.m. only to have the opportunity to kill a huge bear that weighed nearly 300 pounds an hour later. That is a hunt I will not soon forget, and I got to share it all with one of my closest hunting buddies, Hal.

It is not a coincidence that Hal is able to stalk and kill mature Big Woods Bucks. He is successful because he has figured out how to stay on a particular buck's track as long as it takes to catch that buck. Lack of such persistence is what prevents most hunters from capitalizing on buck tracks they find, as if they don't realize there is a buck at the end of that track.

Some hunters are not willing to pay the price, whether it be physical, mental or both, to get an opportunity to kill a buck. Forty-plus years of practice, natural ability, countless mistakes, good decisions and his relentless drive to succeed have contributed to Hal's success. His persistence is intoxicating and has played a significant role in the success his clients have enjoyed killing trophy game animals.

After spending a week chasing mature bucks, I have heard his clients say time and time again, "I learned more about deer, deer hunting and the woods they live in from Hal than I have been able to accumulate in a lifetime of hunting on my own."

The information Hal has provided will help you shorten your learning curve and use some proven techniques and strategies to outsmart, wear down or stack the odds in your favor the next time you hunt what I call the best athlete in the Big Woods: a mature whitetail buck.

Thanks for all the memories, Hal. I look forward to growing old together and facing the challenge of figuring out how to deal with the aches and pains of old age while satisfying our craving to see what is over the next ridge.

-- Chris Dalti, Vice President, Big Woods Bucks, Rhode Island 2009